PRAISE FOR *STRONG LIKE WATER*

"In this riveting story, both heartbreaking and uplifting, Laila Tarraf shows that adversity didn't break her, it awakened her and transformed her into a wise, compassionate leader who manages with strength and tenderness, not having to deny the latter to achieve the former."

—**CARTER CAST**, clinical professor of entrepreneurship at Kellogg School of Management, former CEO of Walmart. com, and author of *The Right (and Wrong) Stuff*

"A deeply insightful book about business and leadership disguised as a devastating memoir about loss and love."

—**JENNIE NASH**, author and founder and CEO of Author Accelerator

"The power of Laila's memoir comes through in her illumination of the trap of hiding in plain sight. When our day-to-day professional lives blind us to who we really are, no one else can see us either. The gift in these pages is that when you see yourself, others will too."

—**DAN ROAM**, author of *The Back of the Napkin* and *Draw to Win*

"Written with striking candor and, yes, heart, Laila Tarraf's story speaks to those grappling with loss and searching for more meaning in work to lead a more balanced, fulfilling life. "

—*MIDWEST BOOK REVIEW*

"*Strong Like Water* highlights a simple truth: we already are spiritual—it's human we're learning how to be."

—**JACQUELYN SMALL**, author of *The Sacred Purpose of Being Human*

"Laila brings forth a compelling memoir that breaks your heart into a million bits and has you cheering at the top of your lungs with her story of love, loss, and renewal in today's world. An amazing first-time debut for an author who brings her personal awakenings to the world of business and leadership. Every page is a precious gift."
—SHERNAZ DAVER, Executive Advisor, Google Ventures (GV)

"This book is a gift—to me, to women, and to the world. I felt myself shift, open, and transform as I turned the pages. I nodded, smiled, and wept, and would need to stop and let myself cry a bit more before continuing on. Joining Laila for this intimate journey has helped me to heal—I am a more whole person for having read her book."
—SUNSHINE YIN, Head of People & Operations, Advanced Digital & Product Team, Bain & Company

"This is a book that EVERY leader needs to read—and that is destined to become a can't-put-it-down classic. *Strong Like Water* casts light on one of the most critical, core workplace questions through a unique and compelling personal narrative. With honesty and insight about her own experiences, Tarraf manages to define head-and-heart leadership and demonstrate exactly what it means to 'bring your whole self to work.' Whether you're just starting your career or leading a large team, in any field or function, *Strong Like Water* points the way to authentic, sustainable success."
—DAISY DOWLING, former Global Head of Talent Development, The Blackstone Group, and author of *Workparent: The Complete Guide to Succeeding on the Job, Staying True to Yourself, and Raising Happy Kids*

"A master class in vulnerability and leadership, this book is a must-read. Equal parts personal narrative and a guidebook for authenticity at work, *Strong Like Water* takes the reader on a full emotional journey as it brilliantly demonstrates what true leadership looks like. So many of us show up to work with outdated ideas of how to be, act, lead. Ms. Tarraf inspires us to throw out the rulebook and forge our own path, from the head to the heart."

—**ANNE ROBIE**, HR Executive and Consultant,
Chief People Officer, Turnitin

STRONG
LIKE
WATER

Published 2021
Printed in the United States of America
Print ISBN: 978-1-64742-022-2
E-ISBN: 978-1-64742-023-9
Library of Congress Control Number: 2020917966

For information, address:
She Writes Press
1569 Solano Ave #546
Berkeley, CA 94707

She Writes Press is a division of SparkPoint Studio, LLC.

Cover and interior design by Tabitha Lahr
Photo of "Young Laila" on page 197 is from the author's family collection

STRONG
LIKE
WATER

*How I Found the Courage
to Lead with Love
in Business and in Life*

LAILA TARRAF

SHE WRITES PRESS

To both my Nadias

My mother and my daughter, who remind me every day that I am part of something bigger; that my strength—our strength as women—extends beyond ourselves.

CONTENTS

Be Like Water

Nothing in the world
is as soft and yielding as water.
Yet for dissolving the hard and inflexible,
nothing can surpass it.
The soft overcomes the hard;
the gentle overcomes the rigid.
Everyone knows this is true,
but few can put it into practice.
Therefore, the Master remains
serene in the midst of sorrow.
Evil cannot enter his heart.
Because he has given up helping,
he is people's greatest help.
True words seem paradoxical.

—LAO TZU-
(Tao Te Ching, chapter 78,
translation by Stephen Mitchell)

Prologue

"Show me a hero and I will write you a tragedy."
—F. Scott Fitzgerald

One of my earliest memories of our life in Beirut was when I was four or five years old. I remember sitting on a tan Moroccan pouf with gold swirls running through it, playing with my baby doll, when I heard scuffling in the nearby dining room. I listened more closely but heard nothing, so I went back to my playing. Soon, however, the scuffling sound returned, accompanied by grunting, and then I started hearing what sounded like someone beating the dust out of the Persian rugs that covered our entryway.

I peered around the corner of the living room wall and saw my parents facing each other, but as I shifted my angle, I could see that their arms were pressed against each other, locked in a sort of stiff embrace.

That's a weird way to hug. Why are they so far apart? I thought.

And then, as my mother unlocked her elbows and their bodies collapsed into each other, I realized that they weren't hugging but rather locked in a physical struggle.

Wait, is my father trying to slap her on the face?

Their arms began to beat back and forth against one another.

Are they fighting? As I got closer, my mother noticed me out of the corner of her eye.

"Get out of here, Laila," she gasped, in between slaps and grunts.

"Mommy, Daddy, stop, stop . . ." I tried to get between them, but I was too short, and their arms flailed about me.

I went back to the pouf and dragged it into the dining room, despite my mother's pleas to leave the room. *I'm not leaving. I'm helping*, I thought.

I went around the dining room table, wedged the pouf between my parents' feet, and climbed up on it. This put me about chest high to them. Not knowing what to do, I threw my arms out to try to stop them. It didn't work. Instead, blows landed on me. Each slap on my body, my arms, brought with it a sharp sting, and I wanted to step down, but I felt so intertwined in their battle that I couldn't think of how to extricate myself.

My face felt hot, and tears welled in my eyes, but just before I began to cry my mother disentangled herself from my father's grip, grabbed me, and ran into the bedroom. As soon as we were alone, I could see that my mother was starting to cry, so I held my tears in. *If we're both crying, who will take care of us?* I thought.

"Don't cry, Mommy. It's okay." I moved into my caregiver role as smoothly and seamlessly as if I had been auditioning for it all my life. The more I soothed her, the less I could feel my pain. Something inside me clicked. *This is good*, I thought. *I'm helping, and I don't have to feel my own pain.* Sitting on the edge of the bed, I patted my mom's hair and hugged her tighter, as if I were the mommy and she were my baby. Soon the satisfaction I felt from breaking up the fight and being able to comfort my mother overrode the stinging red marks on my forearm, and the tears that had threatened to escape from my eyes only moments earlier were nowhere to be found. We heard the front door slam shut, and we both breathed a sigh of relief. Though no words passed between us, it was clear—at least to me—that this was going to be my job in the family.

Most people today who hear of Beirut or Lebanon undoubtedly envision Hezbollah terrorists bombing out buildings and cars, but Beirut in the 1960s was in its heyday—*la belle époque du Liban*.

"There was no better place to be if you worked in finance in the 1960s," a friend once told me. "Every transaction that came out of the Middle East went through Lebanon. The rest of the Middle East was a desert—undeveloped and uneducated at the time. The Lebanese became the de facto financiers for the entire Arab region."

And it was true. Before the start of the 1975 Lebanese civil war, Lebanon, and Beirut as its capital city, was by far the most culturally cosmopolitan place in the Middle East. Christians, Muslims, and Druze lived harmoniously amongst each other. They were united by their national pride, their love of food, family, and above all, la dolce vita.

"Bonjour, how are you, *habibi*?" was, and continues to be, the default greeting in Lebanon—French, English, Arabic—just as every meal begins with a potpourri of small plates of hummus, baba ganoush, and salads made with radishes, cucumbers, tomatoes, and olives fresh from the garden. After World War II, Lebanon gained its independence from France and spent the next two decades building five-star hotels, nightclubs, and beach clubs up and down its Mediterranean coast. The debut of the Casino du Liban at the end of 1959 definitively established Lebanon as the ultimate 1960s destination. The property included a hotel, nightclub, showroom, restaurants, and gaming area. It was set on a cliff about fifteen miles north of Beirut in Jounieh, overlooking a crescent moon–shaped bay. At the time, it was believed to be the most elegant and beautiful casino in the world, and from the beginning it attracted the crème de la crème—Prince Rainier and Princess Grace of Monaco, the Kennedys, Omar Sharif, Brigitte Bardot, and Aristotle Onassis were among its visitors. Pictures I have seen from that era look like a scene out of an old James Bond movie.

This was the Lebanon that my mother and I reentered at the end of 1963 when I was only a baby, a glamorous and hedonistic destination that tantalized all the senses—a small jewel on the Mediterranean containing the magic and authenticity of the East and the occidental culture of the West I had been born into. Sitting on my grandparents' balcony overlooking Beirut and the Mediterranean Sea, the ubiquitous Winston cigarette hanging from her mouth, my mother waited for my father to come find her.

"You can stay here with us, Nadia. You don't need to go back to him," my grandfather tried to reason with his youngest daughter, but my mother would only nod, certain that my father would return for us. She did not want to tell her family that the only reason she agreed to leave Los Angeles and fly back to Beirut was because my father had been deported from the States. She had, in fact, been waiting for him to come home to us in Los Angeles when she learned he had been picked up by an immigration agent while cavorting with friends in Las Vegas, his usual playground.

Soon enough my father showed up at my grandparents' home, turned on the charm offensive, and moved us into a three-story high-rise flat in Achrafieh, a leafy residential district in East Beirut. It wouldn't take long for me to realize that the joie de vivre the rest of Beirut enjoyed during this time stood in stark contrast with the schizophrenic atmosphere inside our new home. There was no joy in our home—ever. The mood vacillated wildly from still and anxious—every clink of a fork or knife breaking a deafening silence before the imminent storm that would eventually crash through our home—to shrill and turbulent, doors slamming and my father yelling, "How many times do I have to tell you not to make a sound before eight a.m.?"

My earliest memory was not an isolated incident; instead, a reoccurring theme in our home became my taking a stance against impending danger, never knowing when I might need to play the hero, to come in and save the day.

CHAPTER 1

BEING RIGHT ISN'T THE POINT

"In the beginner's mind there are many possibilities,
but in the expert's, there are few."
—SHUNRYU SUZUKI

I was hired to be lucky employee #7 at Walmart.com, the Bay Area–based Internet division of Walmart, Inc., in March 2000 at the height of the first Internet bubble. It was a modern-day gold rush, and everyone was convinced they would soon be millionaires. My six months as director of recruiting at Webvan had made me an expert in the burgeoning world of e-commerce. After watching Amazon, Yahoo, Netscape, and AOL pick up steam, Walmart decided that this Internet thing was not going away, and as Internet talent was scarce in the early days, the company decided they needed to be where the talent was. In those days, the talent was in the San Francisco Bay Area. Walmart's corporate headquarters was in Bentonville, Arkansas, a small southern town where Walmart was, by far, the biggest employer and was revered by the community, but I was hired to build the "dot-com" team in San Francisco. In California, Walmart was seen as a corporate pariah and not at all as cool as Internet start-ups that 99 percent of the world had never heard of. I was excited about the challenge.

Trying to convince people to come work for stodgy old Walmart at the height of the Internet bubble was not an easy sell. It may be hard to believe, but people were skeptical of the Fortune One company in the world, even when held up next to an underfunded five-person company with no revenues and no clear future prospects.

"But we're a start-up too," I insisted one day as I appealed to a software engineer who was weighing his options. "Look, we have our own café, and a foosball table on the ground floor," I added, hoping this would show how hip we were.

He looked at me warily, unconvinced. We were a multibillion-dollar, multinational corporation.

Realizing I was losing him, I smiled and said, "Here's the thing, we're the best of both worlds. We're a start-up *and* we're financially backed by the biggest company in the world." And it was true—partially. I had a bigger budget than any other start-up around me at the time, and we *did* take the corporate plane back and forth to Bentonville, even if those planes were tiny, loud six-seaters with no bathrooms on board. It was Walmart, after all.

Those were heady days to be sure and a very surreal time to join the business world. In the mid to late nineties it was hard to distinguish the long-term success probability between the yodeling Yahoooo! and the Pets.com sock puppet. "Dot-com" was on everyone's lips, so much so that a friend's toddler began adding "dot-com" to the end of every sentence. "Mama, can we go to the park dot-com?" *Giggle, giggle.* Everybody was going to get rich. Little did we know that the first dot-com bubble would burst in just a few months, but even after the stock market dropped on that precipitous day on March 10, 2000, our collective irrational exuberance was so deeply rooted that we convinced ourselves this was but a momentary glitch, and we continued hiring like mad, reaching 250 employees by the end of the first year.

As a result, I was asked to take over all of human resources—which initially shocked and insulted me. "What, me? In *human resources*? I'm not an HR person!" To my mind, recruiting was sales—you had to really understand the business and the motivations of your candidate to bring the two together. Hiring the right talent was critical to the business. Human resources, on the other hand, was a downstream function more focused on ticking and tying the administrative details of the business—a pencil pusher, not a visionary. I couldn't even say the word without it feeling heavy on my tongue. HR was where you got sent when you were in trouble. They were the rules-based, uptight, compliance-oriented, school-marmy types. I was a businessperson, for God's sake. *Look, I have an MBA! I'm not some back-office administrator.* Lucky for me, Jeanne Jackson, the CEO of Walmart.com at the time, saw something in me that I did not yet see myself. Like many women who had risen in the business ranks at that time, she was a no-nonsense leader who had little time for my dribbling. "Look, Laila, take the job, and if you don't like it or you're not good at it, you can go back to recruiting." And that was it. She moved on, having much bigger fish to fry.

About six months after I took on the human resources role at Walmart.com, a group of fifteen people sat around a large table at our weekly operating team meeting to discuss that week's priorities. This was one of Jeanne's initiatives, and she led the meetings. As was normal for me at that time, I immediately started getting antsy, wishing that things would go faster. As each person around the table went through their agenda, I found myself getting more and more irritated with the snail-like pace of the meeting.

People, stop asking such stupid questions so we can please just get out of here and go do the work.

Finally, the meeting ended, and as I was making my way out of the room, Jeanne caught my attention and motioned with her finger to follow her into her office. My heart started to pound. *What is this?* I followed her into her office and closed the door.

"If I ever see you doing that again, there will be hell to pay," she said, and stared me down with an intensity I had seen targeted at others, but never at me.

What? What did I do? I was truly in the dark.

"I get it, Laila," she said. "You're smart and quick and you can't be bothered waiting for everyone else. You were rolling your eyes in there, and your body posture was slouched and disrespectful." She paused and got closer. I was frozen in place.

"Let me tell you something: the point is not to be right or to be the first one to get there. The point is to bring everyone along and to get their buy-in. That is the value of those meetings." She went behind her desk, sat down, and reengaged with her computer screen.

I wasn't sure whether I should leave, so I stood there feeling awkward and embarrassed. Finally, she looked up and said, "Don't you ever do that again."

I knew at that point that was my cue to go. I left her office feeling as if I had been struck hard, not fully understanding all she had said, but replaying it over and over in my mind so I wouldn't forget. *What did she mean the point was getting buy-in? I thought the point was to be right and fast.* I could tell when I was impatient, but I had always thought I did a pretty decent job hiding it—apparently not. It would take several more years to understand what she was telling me, and several more after that to really take it to heart. At the time, I was freshly out of business school, eager to prove myself, and working almost exclusively from my head, with no room for anything from the heart. I truly believed there *was* a right way, that I needed to get there faster than anyone, and that this was the path to success and fulfillment.

In my life, I never knew which decisions were going to be the pivotal ones until I looked back at them in the rearview mirror. Taking that HR job was certainly one of them, and it turned out to be a very good one for me professionally. It put me in a functional area that was in the early stages of a transformation, and my foundation in recruiting would serve to make me an expert in the emerging field of talent management. As innovation and technology became more and more important and talent became more and more scarce, companies in the services sector realized that people were the only differentiating factor. From tech to finance, companies were beginning to recognize that an exceptional hire could generate more revenue than a mediocre one by a factor of ten. Over the following twenty years, I moved from being a recruiter to a human resource executive to a leadership coach and a culture carrier.

While I didn't realize it at the time, each step on my career path required me to grow both personally and professionally and to develop the qualities I needed to be successful at each stage. I had innate qualities that served me well—I was quick and smart, and my early years as a recruiter helped me develop an ability to connect with people and discern their true motivation. Unfortunately, the very qualities that made me a good recruiter—fast-talking, results-oriented, always driving for closure—weren't helping me as a newly minted HR vice president. The problem was that I didn't recognize this contradiction within myself. Jeanne's admonishment was my first clue that I was doing something that did not serve me, but I still didn't fully understand what I had done wrong, until two years later when our new CEO, John Fleming, sitting around the same conference table, said something very similar to a group of us in our weekly operating team meeting.

"John, those guys in Bentonville don't understand what's happening out here. We need to do things differently to compete with all these start-ups that are popping up every week. They're slowing us down with all their constraints!"

"I get it, guys, we need to move fast, but I learned a long time ago that being right is rarely the point. We need to slow down and spend time investing in our relationship with our key partners at the Home Office."

I immediately recalled Jeanne's reprimand of me. But I still thought that being right was exactly the point, even if I had learned to keep my eye-rolling to a minimum. I couldn't imagine how I could have this so backwards. It would take me twenty years to realize that having the right answer—a goal I was constantly after as a student and young executive—does nothing to bring people together to work on complex problems. And as a leader it only serves to shame your team and prevent them from taking risks, which is the death knell for any sort of innovation or creativity. At the time, however, this was completely counterintuitive to me. I had been a lifelong overachiever who used achievement as a way to get my parents' attention because it was, in fact, the only way they noticed me.

I had always been told that my newly married Lebanese parents were able to obtain U.S. visas and move to Los Angeles in the early 1960s because my mother had been working at the American embassy in Beirut and was able to procure student visas for the two of them to study and live abroad. They had moved to a town called Inglewood, a small suburb southwest of Los Angeles close to the airport. It didn't take long before my mother was pregnant, but their young marriage was already showing signs of wear. My father, it seemed, could not be contained. Unlike my mother, who had been a very strong student in school, my father didn't share her passion for learning. No, George Tarraf was above all that schoolwork. He was going to make it big on his own. Soon, he quit school and began making the five-hour drive to Las Vegas to visit an old childhood friend who had recently moved there from Lebanon.

His weekend jaunts became more and more frequent until he eventually stopped coming home altogether. At her wit's end, my mother phoned her older brother, Mitri, who was living in Fresno, to ask for help. Mitri had moved to the States a few years before my parents, married an American, and began teaching psychology at Fresno State University. Eight years older than my mother, he was like a father to her.

"Nadia, come live with us here in Fresno. We will take care of you."

"You know I can't do that . . . What if George comes back and I'm not in Los Angeles?"

My uncle ultimately acquiesced and called his brother-in-law, Leo, and asked if my mother could live with him and his wife until a longer-term solution could be found.

I have never been able to find out if my mother was alone when she gave birth to me. In fact, I don't know if my father had ever returned during those first few months of my life. My mother quit school and got a job so that she could help pay rent for the room she and I shared in Leo and his wife's home. While Leo and his wife were very kind to my mother and loved having a baby in the house, my mother soon learned that Leo's wife could not have children and as they began to ask if my mother would consider allowing them to adopt me, an uneasiness crept into their relationship and she knew she could not stay for long.

My mother heard less and less from my father over the months, but she was so overjoyed and overwhelmed in raising a baby alone, she didn't dwell too long on my father's obvious disinterest. Meanwhile, my uncle in Fresno continued to ask her to move up to live with his family while my grandfather in Beirut began exerting greater pressure on my mother to return home to Lebanon. She had resisted my grandfather's insistence that she return home several times over the previous year when he had learned of my father's frequent trips to Las Vegas, for work—nothing more—she had assured my grandfather, lying to herself as much as to him.

"Beirut is your home; come home and be with your family. *Yallah*, we are waiting for you," her father continued to insist.

In the fall, when I was nine months old, my mother learned that my father had been deported. "I'm sorry to tell you, Nadia, that immigration came for George this morning. He's been sent back to Lebanon," his buddy had said. This was all my mother needed to hear to finally allow her father to send her the money needed to buy a ticket to fly back to Beirut.

My mother and I moved in with my grandparents and enjoyed the comfort and safety that comes with returning home and being with family, despite my grandfather's continued insistence that my mother not to go back to my father.

"Nadia, this man will make life difficult for you. Stay here with us. We will take care of you and Laila."

But Beirut was a small town, and so it wasn't long before my father was able to make his way back into our lives. Unable to resist my father's charm, my mother soon reunited with him, and in three years' time they had had two more children. One of my parents' friends confided in me once, "Sweetie, your parents' relationship was very complicated. One day, honey; one day, onion." He twisted his wrist in one direction and then the other, mimicking the back and forth between the two. "Your mother was a goody two-shoes, and George knew he could win her back every time."

During our seven years in Beirut, my father spoke often of returning to America. We would walk along the Avenue de Paris, a wide seaside promenade overlooking Raouché with its two large rocks jutting out of the Mediterranean Sea, and I would ask my father, "When are we going to America, Daddy?" His answer was always the same. "*Bookrah*." Tomorrow.

Tomorrow finally came when my uncle Mitri's petition to bring his extended family to America was accepted. In May of 1971, my mother's side of the family was able to move back to the States. The seven years my parents had been in Beirut had seen the political climate shift dramatically. After the 1967 Palestinian/ Israeli conflict, even more Palestinians came into Lebanon, which further increased the number of refugees in the country. Over time, these refugees wanted more power, and factions and alliances began to develop between the Muslim Palestinians and the Muslim Lebanese. It soon became evident that a civil war between the Christian and the Muslim residents of the country was brewing, but like all political matters within the tiny state of Lebanon, there were bigger players involved—Syria just north and east of Lebanon supported the Muslims, while Israel to the south, as the other religious minority in the Middle East, supported the Christian militia. We were lucky to leave when we did because a civil war lasting fifteen years erupted just a few years after our departure.

My family and I first landed in Fresno, where my uncle Mitri and his family lived. My father quickly took stock of his work prospects in this dusty, central Californian town and decided to move us immediately to another dusty town, one where he implicitly knew he would have more opportunity to be successful: Las Vegas. He knew his six years working at the Casino du Liban would give him an edge, and he was right. We moved into a small two-bedroom apartment on Birthday Street, not far from the Strip, where my father quickly got a job at one of the casinos downtown a few miles away. After a few months there, he had proven himself a competent blackjack and craps dealer and was able to get a croupier job at the Stardust Hotel. Two years later, he landed a coveted position at the prestigious Sands, where he built a career over the following twenty years, working until the last day the casino was open before it was scheduled to be demolished in 1996 to make way for the big mega-casinos that were going up during that time.

He never did return to Beirut, permanently burying all his childhood memories—those of his disciplinarian father, his younger brother's mysterious suicide—and the atrocities that were to be committed over the following fifty years to the jewel of a country he used to call home.

———————————

Not surprisingly, my parents had a very traditional marriage—Mom was a homemaker; Dad, the breadwinner. Their roles were static, and they fought constantly about big things and little. It was easy to love my mother. She was so kind and nurturing; there was nothing she wouldn't do for you. But while my father had a temper, there was also a tenderness about him. He was a hard man, a force of nature as unpredictable as the weather, and yet, to me, he often had a look on his face like he had a secret, the corner of his mouth turned up in a half-smile, a gleam in his eye. And when he held me, I could see that he loved me despite his dark moods, which he regularly laid upon my mother.

As the eldest of three children, I quickly took on the role of the mediator between my warring parents and my younger brother and sister. I became the bridge between two cultures, two languages, and two very different ways of being—one tough and unbending, the other kind but with no agency. I learned to never be vulnerable, to never be needy, to never be soft, and above all, to never ask for anything. My strength became my power, so it was only natural that when I started working, I was drawn to roles that recreated the need to bring opposing sides together. Bridging the interests of employees with that of a company seemed natural to me, and for seven years, I learned the function of HR and was part of building a very special culture at Walmart.com.

After seven years at Walmart.com, I realized that in order for me to grow in my career, I would have to move to Bentonville, Arkansas. And as much as I had grown to appreciate my more conservative brethren in Bentonville, San Francisco was my home. So, when a headhunter called to say that Peet's Coffee and Tea, located right over the Bay Bridge in Emeryville, California, was searching for a chief people officer, I was intrigued.

Coffee is one of the few beverages that seems to bridge people and cultures, I thought. Millions of people around the world begin their day over a cup of coffee. Its ubiquitous presence made it somehow part of the intimacy and connection I had been searching for my whole life.

I would soon learn the story of how Alfred Peet moved to Berkeley in 1966, opening the first Peet's Coffee and Tea on the corner of Walnut and Vine, just a stone's throw from the University of California at Berkeley, my alma mater. Having immigrated from the Netherlands, Alfred Peet was appalled by the poor quality of coffee and tea in the United States in the age of Maxwell House and Folgers. He arrived in Berkeley during a special time and played a seminal role in the creation of the "gourmet ghetto" alongside Alice Waters, owner of Chez Panisse, and others who began the movement toward fresh, all-natural, and local.

Alfred Peet's dedication to his craft and his singular focus on coffee, tea, and spices made him a master at sourcing, blending, and roasting only the highest quality beans by hand. In the process, he spawned the specialty coffee movement in the United States. Several small micro-roasters apprenticed under Mr. Peet, and the first Starbucks store in Seattle actually sold Peet's beans. This was the man who really started the coffee revolution, and I wanted desperately to be part of the story. It felt like more than just a job; it felt like I could be part of an important piece of history with a responsibility to carry on the legacy of this important man and be part of the movement going forward. Unlike the start-ups all around us that were created and disappeared in a matter of years or even months, the Peet's brand was a living, breathing thing that required tender care and feeding, and I took my responsibility as a brand steward very seriously.

It was the sort of commitment I was sorely in need of because I had struggled with commitment my whole life. Before meeting my husband, Daniel, my friends used to call me the runaway bride because I'd had two serious relationships each lasting almost three years, and in each I was the one who ultimately walked away. The first was with a man who was much like my father, very controlling and dominant, whom I used to spar with constantly. When I heard he was shopping for a ring, I knew I could not spend my life with a man like that, so I broke it off. The relationship after him was with a loving, kind man who, unfortunately, I felt I could control. I didn't want to have that much power, so after a two-year engagement during which I was unable to settle on a wedding date, he asked for the ring back. I felt a little like Goldilocks, swinging from one type of man to another, searching for the one that was "just right." By the time I met Daniel—a younger man who pursued me with a school boy's vigor—I was so disconnected from my feelings, I could no longer hear what my heart was telling me, so I made a rational, head-based decision and chose to marry him. In 2004, we had our first child, a precious girl we named Nadia.

She was a whisper of a thing, small and delicate, hardly bigger than a small puppy. I was on cloud nine and held her in my arms or against my chest in the Baby Bjorn most of her waking hours. Daniel used to joke that between me and my mother, Nadia's feet had never graced the ground. She was indeed a very late walker. No matter, I was deeply in love for the first time in my life. We toggled through a couple of nannies before we found Marci Nelson, who ended up moving downstairs into the large bonus room we later built out into a separate in-law apartment for her. Over the next ten years Marci would become Nadia's nanny and my right hand in more ways than I could have ever imagined in those early days. I went back to work and when I got the Peet's call, I felt confident I was ready for the next big thing with the home front in good hands.

My early observations were that the employees at Peet's seemed to have a heartfelt connection to the company. These were not people afraid of commitment, and their passion for coffee and team was palatable. It was part of why I was so excited about interviewing for the role at Peet's: I wanted that in my life. I just didn't know how to articulate it. On paper, however, I had few of the necessary qualifications—experience working with an hourly workforce, employment law, geographically dispersed employees. Why did they even want to meet with me? I was concerned the headhunter might have oversold me, but I thought there was no harm in going out and getting some good interview experience.

I met Pat O'Dea, the CEO of Peet's Coffee and Tea, on a cold, damp day in October of 2006. The day did not start well. Instead of going to the corporate headquarters in Emeryville, I went to the local Peet's coffee shop in Emeryville instead. Strike one. After I had realized my mistake, I called the recruiter, who called Pat's assistant. I was told to stay put and he would come to meet me at the store.

Oh man, what a rookie he must think I am. I can't even figure out how to get to the damn interview. I sat there nervously ingesting the perfectly blended rocket fuel Peet's was so well known for, feeling more and more like an imposter with each passing minute. Finally, a tall man with dark hair graying around the temples walked in the door. He caught my eye and asked, "Laila?"

I stood up and shook his hand. "Yes, hello, Pat, nice to meet you. Sorry about the mix-up with the locations."

He smiled, looking me in the eye. "No problem, honest mistake. I see you've already got something to drink." He indicated toward my half-empty cup. "Well, let's sit down, shall we?"

Over the following hour, he pelted me with questions, rarely breaking eye contact with me. After the first few minutes, a strange calm came over me, and I decided I was just going to do the best I could and let the chips fall where they may. Later, Pat would tell me it was my answer to two questions that convinced him it was worth the risk to hire someone who had only had human resources experience at a Silicon Valley tech start-up, even if that start-up was a division of the biggest retailer in the world.

"How would you go about determining what kind of benefits we should have at Peet's?"

I took a sip of my coffee and looked off into the distance, gathering my thoughts. Here was my chance to get the answer "right," to show that despite lacking the necessary experience on paper, I was fully capable of figuring it out. "Well, I guess I would find out which companies we compete with for talent, benchmark what they have, and then hire a benefits broker that could do a cost-benefit analysis, so we could pick the best plan." Pause. "Right? I mean, I've never done it, but that seems to make sense." I smiled and laughed nervously.

He gave me no feedback whatsoever. Strike two?

"Okay," he continued, "what would you do if you had an employee who was threatening to unionize? Like a part-time barista working in the Santa Cruz store."

I breathed deeply and leaned in, saying, "First, you have to realize that would be my greatest fear."

No response.

I put myself into that position and thought for a few moments, again searching for the answer that would make me sound like a confident, no-nonsense business leader. Finally, I said, "I would probably do two things; first, I would call an attorney to get legal advice, and second, I would go down to the store to find out for myself what was going on."

I walked out of the store believing that I had fully bombed the interview, but the next day the recruiter told me that Pat thought I was perfect for the job.

"Why?" I asked.

"Because he thinks you're smart and you have good judgment and you can learn the parts of HR you don't know."

It was more proof that the rational, confident, strong, and capable persona was the one who always won. It didn't matter that I didn't know what I was talking about; what mattered was that I was quick and decisive, no-nonsense and goal-oriented. I was ready to jump into my new job and double down on that way of being in the world.

CHAPTER 2

WHERE YOU STAND DEPENDS
ON WHERE YOU SIT

"The question is not what you look at, but what you see."
—HENRY DAVID THOREAU

I started at Peet's in December of 2006, and soon my work life seemed to be firing on all cylinders. I went from being the pariah at cocktail parties where the response to my working at Walmart. com was usually met with a thinly veneered air of judgment to being everybody's best friend—*Oh my gosh, you run HR at Peet's? I love Peet's!* The interesting thing was that while Walmart's culture was extremely right-leaning and Peet's was left, the cultural challenges at both companies were virtually identical. I started to realize that while a strong culture gives you a strong sense of identity, it also serves to divide you and give you very legitimate reasons for not continuing to evolve, which for any company will eventually be the kiss of death. I heard the same words come out of my tattooed barista as I did my God-fearing store manager at the Bentonville home office. "That's just the way we do it here." Conversely, I went from being that crazy left-wing San Francisco HR lady who had all these wild employee-friendly ideas to that corporate, mass-market HR person who was bound to turn us into Starbucks overnight. Pat used to say, "Where you stand depends on where you sit," and those words echoed in my mind just about every day as we tried to move Peet's from a sleepy regional premium coffee retail company to a multichannel coffee producer with a diverse workforce.

I thought I was a coffee person when I started working at Peet's. I was mistaken on so many levels. The depth of reverence and passion that the employees had for coffee—for Peet's coffee— was close to sacred. It was a way of life, a way of being, and was a real differentiator in our culture. We regularly referred to Alfred Peet as the grandfather of specialty coffee—not just the founder of our company but the grandfather of *all* specialty coffee. This was a responsibility and an honor our Peetniks—the nickname that was given to Peet's employees in deference to the beatniks from the 1960s Berkeley movement—took very seriously. Our roots were deep, and our founder's ethos was as strong and present in 2006 as it was in 1966. We were coffee purists, and we worshipped at the altar of the bean.

We used to have long and passionate debates about whether we could only hire people who were passionate about coffee or if we could hire people, like myself, who were passionate about other things in their lives and who could then develop a passion for Peet's. I loved my work, and in that first year I was lucky enough to build one of the best teams I have ever worked with. In my first six months, I made three strategic hires and elevated a couple of folks on my team to meet the daunting business challenges we faced. It felt great to be a strong part of a strong team, doing what I felt was important work for an iconic Bay Area brand.

But despite having enough caffeine to wake up an entire nation, I was in fact living in the darkest night. While my professional life was soaring, my personal life was sputtering and gasping for air. I had a beautiful three-year-old girl at home—one I had longed for my whole life—but my marriage was already feeling wobbly.

Daniel and I squabbled over the tiniest things, and it was getting harder and harder to connect with him with any sort of intimacy. Early one Saturday morning, only a few months after Nadia was born, I was getting her dressed and setting her up in her swing when Daniel rolled out of bed and shuffled into the kitchen. I feared he would be grumpy, as he so often was those days.

"Good morning. How'd you sleep?" I asked, purposefully trying to show concern and care.

"I feel terrible; I just want to go back to bed," he replied.

"Do you want to go to the park with us? It's really nice out, and I thought we could take her outside before she has to take a nap."

"Do I look like I want to go to the park?" His tone was so derisive, it knocked me back on my heels.

I felt an anger rise within.

"Listen," I said, crossing the living room and coming into the kitchen to face him. "I don't know what the hell is going on, but you need a serious reality check here." I ignored his sneer and continued. "Take a look around. It does not get any better than this, right here, right now." Looking him in the eye, I softened my voice and uttered, "You have a beautiful, healthy daughter, a wife who loves you and cares about you, a beautiful home in an amazing city. This is it." I paused and looked at him for some sort of recognition, some acknowledgment, but all I saw was his deadpan stare reflecting back at me. I finished by almost whispering, "This is what everyone works for their entire lives, and you have it right now." I wanted to yell, "GET HAPPY, DAMNIT," but instead I quietly muttered, "You can go ahead and be unhappy if you want, but I will not allow you to take away my joy." And with that, I turned from him and finished preparing Nadia to go in her stroller.

Later, neither of us even mentioned the exchange, one of many to come. My personal and professional lives began to diverge, and I couldn't bear to admit my dirty little secret, even to myself: the chief people officer—the people expert—was struggling with her own personal connections to people.

Six months after I started at Peet's, Daniel walked into our bedroom and suddenly announced he would be moving out.

"I'm leaving," he said calmly as he leaned against the bedroom doorframe. "I know *you* never really loved *me*, so I'm going now."

I was sitting on our bed sorting through some mail, and it took a moment for what he had said to fully sink in. I looked up at him, confused, unable to say anything. *You're leaving? You mean for the afternoon? For the night? What do you mean, you're leaving?* I searched his eyes for more information, but none came, so I just sat there, my mouth open, my heart racing as I watched him walk out the door. Instead of fire alarms ringing and moving me into action, I did what I do so well: I pretended everything was fine—to myself and to my family and friends. *Nothing to see here, folks; move along. I've got this whole thing under control.*

This was in July of 2007, one week before we were to go to Sun Valley for the Fourth of July wedding of a close friend, a wedding in which Daniel was singing. Over the next few days he took a few things with him, strategically coming home when I wasn't there so we wouldn't run into each other. Ever so slowly, it began to sink in that this was really happening. I couldn't bring myself to go to the wedding without him that week, so I called my girlfriend to apologize and to tell her that Daniel would not be able to sing at her wedding.

"What happened?" she asked.

"I'm honestly not sure," I replied, still shocked and dumbfounded. I allowed the awkward silence to take up the space between us, refusing to offer any additional information about the change of plans or what had precipitated it.

"I'm so sorry," I finally said, and quietly hung up the phone.

I decided to take Nadia to visit my parents in Las Vegas for the holiday weekend. I never said a word to them, or anyone, about what had just happened. It was as if I was incapable of processing this news and couldn't fathom how to begin to explain it, so instead I stayed very still, hoping it might just go away. Perhaps this was why I chose to go to home. While I may have been tempted to confide in a friend to help me process what had just happened, there was no chance of this happening with my family. Everything was always fine on the surface for us—until it wasn't. Being in Las Vegas with my family allowed me to more easily recoil from the truth. I felt myself closing in, battening down the hatches and pulling in the drawbridge in anticipation of the storm I subconsciously knew I would be facing soon.

I hadn't kept in touch with friends from high school, so my trips to Vegas often made me feel lonelier and more isolated. As I watched Nadia play in the plastic pool my mother had bought for her, I thought back on my childhood and how quickly we had all assimilated into American culture. We enrolled in many of the after-school activities that our friends were in—soccer, basketball, dance—and I quickly mastered the art of being American during the day while maintaining my Lebanese identity in the evening: pizza and hamburgers for lunch, kibbe and hummus for dinner. During the day I heard only English, and during the evenings only Arabic: Lebanese on the inside and American on the outside. My uncle shared with me once that despite the family's initial concern that we could not speak English when we arrived in Las Vegas, within six months all three of us forgot all our Arabic and spoke only English.

My mother signed me up for ballet after school, and I quickly became friends with the two blonde girls everybody liked in my class, Sharon and Jennifer. Our ballet teacher was Jennifer's mom who, incidentally, used to dance with the Folies Bergere at the Tropicana Hotel. She wore a T-shirt that said, "Feel protected tonight, sleep with a cop," which my mother thought was scandalous.

"Mom, Jenny's dad is a cop. It's sort of a joke," I tried to explain.

My mother only nodded when I shared this piece of news with her, asking "So, why does she have to tell us about it?" I had no response for this question.

Sharon, Jennifer, and I would go to each other's houses often and hang out by the pool when the weather was hot. We would play music, and I would make up stories about our lives, reciting them out loud as if I were reading them from a book. Of course, the protagonist was always one of us —or all of us—and there was usually a love interest, one of the boys we had a crush on at school, and a villain—a mean girl or a teacher—but they always had a happy ending.

At home, I was usually successful in staying on my father's good side—I was always on my mother's good side. I knew that doing well in school would assure me positive attention from both my parents but especially from my father.

"Dad, look, I got my report card today and I got straight A's. An A+ in math!"

He would take the paper from my hand, look it up and down, then smile at me and say, "Very good job, Laila." I would savor these small acknowledgments of my academic accomplishments and try to recall them on the days my dad's mood was stormier.

I didn't really understand what was happening between my mother and my father at the time, how much my mother protected us from my father's anger. Even on my father's dark days, I could see something deep within him that was yearning for love. He reminded me of a lion with a thorn in his paw, growling fiercely out of pain, and I believed if I could overcome my fear and get close to the lion, he would let me take out the thorn and we would be friends. Years later when I watched the movie *Good Will Hunting*, something deep within me knew that my father was Will, a beautiful boy who had been crushed by his father and was too proud to admit he was in pain. Pride was the deadly sin that afflicted the Tarraf family right down to me, but inside I saw the hurt boy, so I continually tried to approach the lion, my heart feeling like it was outside my body, beating wildly, as I willed myself to move closer and closer as if to say, *I see you; don't hurt me. I'm like you. I'm strong.*

My life quickly bifurcated—life in the home and life outside. Inside our home, I was always wary and hypervigilant, trying to anticipate the next eruption. Each weekday morning, I woke very early, made myself a bowl of cereal, and slid the box over to my brother and sister on the kitchen counter. I put on my blue-and-yellow pinstriped plaid skirt, put my long, brown hair into pigtails, and only at the last minute would I tiptoe into my mother and father's room to wake up my mother so she could drive me to school. Those last few moments each morning when I had to enter the lion's den terrified me because I knew the consequences if I were to wake my father. Making my way around the bed to get to my mother's side, I would kneel by her head and gently nudge her so that she could drive us to school.

"Mommy, it's time to leave," I would whisper, and as she climbed out of bed, I would take advantage of the rustling of the sheets to make my way back out of the room again.

My mother picked my father up from work every night at seven o'clock. Those few hours after school were heaven for us because we could just be kids, make noise, eat wherever we wanted in the house, and not worry about getting in trouble. My mother's lenient parenting style stood in stark contrast to that of my father's, or perhaps that was her way of counterbalancing my father's extreme brand of discipline. When Dad wasn't home, it was a free-for-all, and we loved it. After Mom returned from picking up Dad from work, I would gauge the situation to determine if it was safe to hang out in the den and watch TV or if Dad seemed like he was in a nasty mood, in which case I would head directly to my room saying I had a lot of homework I needed to finish.

School came easily to me, but learning to fit in socially was more of a challenge. When I turned nine years old, my father took the three of us down to the barber and gave us all short boy's haircuts. As I got out of the barber chair, my father lifted my chin with his hand.

"You'll thank me for this as the weather gets hotter," he said.

I nodded and pulled on the strands that barely covered my neck, smiling up at him, pushing down the tears. Sure enough, the following Saturday as the temperature climbed into the triple digits, a group of kids began to run through a sprinkler that a neighbor had turned on. I felt free with my new short hair and threw off my shirt to run around in my shorts with the others. Soon, I saw the kids around me whisper and giggle. I didn't know what was so funny. *Are they laughing at me? What am I doing?* My stomach started to hurt, and my body began to buzz. Something was wrong, but I didn't know what.

Then I overheard one of the kids say, "Is that a boy or a girl?" and point at me.

What? What's wrong with these people; can't they see I'm a girl? It must be my hair.

It would be years before I realized that it was not my hair that confused them as to my gender, though it probably didn't help. No one had told me that in the United States, nine-year-old girls—even ones who looked like nine-year-old boys—had to keep their shirts on to play.

I let out a soft laugh as I recalled the early days of my youth and cringed thinking about myself running around without a top, not having a clue as to what was so funny. I distinctly remembered how awful it felt not to be able to tell my mom, knowing she wouldn't understand, and then I realized that I still felt the same way, only the stakes were higher.

———————

Throughout the summer, Daniel came and went with his self-proclaimed, newfound freedom. It was unlike me not to hold his feet to the fire, to demand an explanation from him for his behavior, but I was emotionally exhausted at this point in our marriage. We had struggled to have Nadia and had been trying to have a second child, and I just didn't have it in me to engage with whatever little crisis he was going through in that moment. *I'm so tired of being the therapist, the voice of reason, the cheerleader, the fixer,* I thought. *I need to focus on my child and on myself right now, so I'm just going to let this one play out for a while.*

I focused on my work the rest of the summer and prepared for Nadia to begin her first day of preschool at the Jewish Community Center. The JCC used the Reggio Emilia pedagogy, which focused on a child-centered approach to teaching rather than seeing children as empty vessels who needed to be filled with knowledge. The idea that the curricula would be inspired by the children was very much in alignment with my philosophy on learning and life: keep the external rules to a minimum and tap into what excites and motivates people internally. When the first day of school came, I watched my fairylike three-year-old walk toward the big red wooden gates on a leafy block of Arguello Street. She was hardly bigger than the Paul Frank lunch box she carried at her side. As I was lingering outside of her classroom struggling to turn around and leave, Daniel showed up. I realized he must not have expected me to be there so late and was waiting for me to leave. I was surprised by how awkward it was to see him, given that I had not seen much of him since he'd announced his departure a couple of months earlier. He seemed so sad, leaning against the preschool door, gazing at Nadia from afar. I had to talk to him. I approached him and asked if we could please go somewhere and talk about what was going on. He reluctantly agreed, and we went to a small coffee shop on Clement Street.

It was one of those quintessentially San Francisco summer mornings, heavy fog with so much mist in the air it felt like spit on your face. I noticed my mind grasping for something, anything banal to anchor on so I wouldn't have to feel the anxiety building inside me. We sat in front of our old-style diner coffee cups, the air between us thick and viscous, and struggled to look each other in the eye.

"What's going on?" I asked. "Where have you been?" I tried to sound casual, but inside I was bracing myself for what he might say. He looked upset, his brows furrowed, his normally nicely coiffed hair unwashed and falling in his eyes, his face unshaven. As he looked up I saw he had tears in his eyes.

"My friends think I'm crazy," he said. "They say I have everything a guy could want, a nice house, a loving and successful wife, a beautiful healthy baby, what more could I want?"

I was taken aback; I hadn't expected this. But rather than relief, I felt myself hardening. For the past couple of months, he had been so angry, accusing me of not loving him and blaming me for his actions. I was not expecting a teary-eyed, repentant Daniel. In that moment, I saw that he was sorry for leaving and that he was asking to come back. My heart constricted like a lemon squeezed of its last drops. I wanted to believe him, but I could see that he was lost, had gotten himself out to sea, and was asking for a line back to shore. But I didn't want to be his rescuer, or his savior. I felt the insidious pull I had always felt in our relationship, combined with an icy-hot guilt that washed over me as I resisted the pull to help him. I felt a foreshadowing dread and somehow knew if I took him back in that moment that we would be here again and again. I couldn't do it; I felt heavy, resolved, but didn't have the courage to say so out loud. So I stayed silent. I didn't throw out the lifeline and soon he stopped talking, realizing I wasn't going to offer him safe passage back into the harbor. I left him out there on that cold, foggy day to handle the storms that he was steering himself into, alone and ill-equipped. A few weeks later, he moved out of our home for good and into his own apartment.

Throughout October and November, I tried to wrap my head around my new reality. Unless I interceded, our seven-year marriage was heading toward a very quick and sudden end. And yet I was incapable of fully engaging with the reality of my situation. It was as if I expected someone to jump out from behind the proverbial curtain and yell, "Just kidding!" I willed myself to stay above it all, as if it were not happening, and I was very good at talking myself into this alternative reality. *Maybe if I stay very quiet, this whole thing will just pass by me and I won't have to acknowledge any of it,* my inner voice said. In the end, my attempt to live in this alternate universe failed, and I was truly shocked when Daniel started making plans to file for divorce. I also learned that Daniel had taken a leave of absence from his enterprise sales job at T-Mobile. Evidently, the apparent stress of our separation had made it difficult for him to focus on work. He was now completely untethered from real life with no daily responsibilities of a wife, a child, or a job. I knew in my bones that this was not good for him, but I blocked this feeling out and dutifully went to work every day.

Ironically, the worse my personal life got, the stronger I was at work. It was as if all my pent-up fears fueled my manic drive for achievement at work. I became even more intense and more willful, driving for results. The timing was good because the company needed help. By October, nine months into my tenure at Peet's, it felt as if we were performing open-heart surgery on the company. Pat had been the CEO of Peet's for five years, focused on growing top-line revenues by opening up new stores and moving into other sales channels like grocery stores and wholesale. He had pushed the organization as far as it could go, and by the time he hired me, there was a lot of work to be done. Five years of growth without a dedicated focus on HR resulted in many people over their heads and underqualified for the roles they held. There was little process, and most of the knowledge of how things worked was held in the heads of long-tenured "Peetniks" who were not aware of how their part fit into the overall picture. Shifting the organization from one where tribal knowledge ruled to one that had clear roles and responsibilities was a big challenge, and I was never sure if changing one thing in one part of the organization would break something else on the other side of the building. Right about the time Daniel moved out of our home, I was knee-deep in a big restructure where we had torn apart the existing retail support team and were in the process of creating a centralized training and communication function within the human resources department that could support all the channels of business, not just retail. It was messy, meaty work and just what I needed to focus my energy and keep my mind off my own personal crisis at home.

But the truth wanted to come out despite my best efforts to keep it under wraps. One day, as I finished a particularly long meeting with Pat, I surprised myself by telling him that Daniel and I had separated. Tears came to my eyes, but I swallowed hard and pushed them back down again. Pat took my cue and veered the conversation back to work. A few weeks later, I was out with friends when they asked me what the latest news was with our separation. I told them that I wasn't sure, that communication was erratic, mostly focused on trying to find times when Daniel could see Nadia, but that even these visits were short because he was always distracted. I could tell he was drinking more despite his attempts at hiding it, and I suspected he might have started to do drugs, but as I had always minimized Daniel's excessive behavior, above all to myself, I wasn't willing to go there just yet. I was afraid of what I would find, and I had lost the will to be a party to this battle. I didn't know if this was my core survival instinct in the face of imminent danger or my maternal instinct trying to shield my daughter from the impending fallout, but I felt a resolve and a heaviness that was immovable. This was not my fight. I would not—could not—save him. I had been the grown-up in the relationship far too long; our marriage was an anchor for him. I couldn't imagine how he was going to manage things on his own. My friends speculated that I was right and that he would probably move back to South Dakota, but I couldn't see how he would have the wherewithal to make that kind of move. I started to feel him slipping away. Everyone dismissed this idea, and I wanted so desperately to believe them, that I willed myself into another alternate reality: I told myself everything was fine, that it wasn't my problem, and pushed the worry down.

A week later, I asked Daniel's sister to come up to San Francisco to spend time with Nadia around Halloween. She would stay longer to look after Nadia while I went to a wedding in Mexico for a few days. I told her that Daniel and I had separated and that things were not good between us. Daniel and Stephanie had always been close, and I had hoped that she could be a positive influence on her big brother. While Stephanie was staying with us, Daniel was supposed to take Nadia to the daddy-daughter dance at the St. Francis Yacht Club—a sweet event they had gone to the year before that he was eager to recreate—but when he came to pick her up, it was clear he was under the influence of something. His face was puffy, and he was sweating and agitated. *What the hell is this?* I thought. This was more than drinking. This felt like something much more dangerous. Pain pills? Cocaine? Was I being irresponsible in letting him take Nadia with him? I resisted my instinct to keep her home only because she was dressed up in her maroon velvet dress, her hair tied back in a bow, all ready for her date. I didn't want to break her heart; she was so excited to see her daddy. I was tormented by this decision, unable to look Daniel in the eye, so clear was his altered state.

I ultimately acquiesced because Stephanie assured me that she would look out for Nadia and drive them to the yacht club herself. I held my breath until Nadia returned home hours later, safe and sound. I knew things were bad, but Stephanie's reaction to Daniel seemed calm, so I convinced myself that she knew better and that it would be all right.

Much later Stephanie confided in me that she was surprised at the state she had found her brother in. She told me that she had had a serious talk with him, but that Daniel had begged her not to say anything to me, so I remained blissfully, willfully ignorant to how bad things had gotten. Stephanie left a few days later. It was the last time she would see her brother alive.

Chapter 3

LESS TALK, MORE ACTION

"The mind is the place where the soul
goes to hide from the heart."
—Michael Singer

I didn't realize how big and thick the wall I had constructed to divide my personal and professional life had become. The events that were hurtling toward me that year would create a fissure in that wall, which would eventually allow a pinprick of light to begin to shine into the dark, unexamined places of my mind. But at the time, I wasn't exactly welcoming that change. I used every coping mechanism in my well-stocked arsenal to keep myself compart-mentalized and separate from my fear. Subconsciously throwing myself into work was a go-to distraction for me. It gave me a very real and highly productive outlet for the fear and anxiety that were bubbling up inside of me—and fortunately, there was a lot of work that needed to be done.

Peet's had more than doubled its store count over the previous five years without any real organization or planning, and there were as many ways of running each store as there were stores themselves. Pat insisted that we needed to provide a consistent operating standard across all stores, but the company had struggled with exactly how to put this in place. I became consumed with trying to develop what we called our Retail Operating Philosophy, or ROP. I wanted to create something simple and dazzling—to hit the ball out of the park. I turned to my friend Dan Roam, who was an expert in visual communication, to help me solve this knotty problem.

After a few working meetings in October, Dan presented a framework that looked like a bento box. It very clearly showed how Peet's vision, mission, and values tied to the four key focus areas that we identified for each store manager: serving customers, managing the operations, developing their people, and inspiring employees, customers, and communities. It was ingenious in its simplicity. In one glance, a new barista could understand how her responsibilities tied to the broader vision and mission of the company. Just as importantly, the framework gave us a way to tie all the training and communication materials we were building out back to these core responsibilities, which in turn tied back to the company's vision and mission. We had built a puzzle with interlocking pieces, and over the next few years we focused on building out the training modules that supported the main components of this system.

Years later, Dan would share with me that he was shocked to learn what I had been living through personally during this time because he never saw an inkling of it in our professional working relationship. We worked very closely for several months, in person and on the phone, and he had no clue that my marriage was in trouble, that my relationship with my parents was a wreck, that I had no one I would allow myself to turn to for help. I had two lives, two selves. While my personal life was falling apart, I was cementing my reputation as a get-things-done executive who could excel at work, not just in HR but across the organization. I became Pat's go-to on all major initiatives, and this fed my desire to be needed. I didn't notice that being needed at work was a highly respectable and valid way to maintain control and keep my own needs hidden, above all to myself.

Pat would tell me later that he really didn't understand half of what I was saying during that first year but decided he would allow me to run on my own for a while as it looked like I was getting results. Later, I realized what a gift this was because I could see that Pat did not extend this same level of autonomy to the head of sales or marketing, and they routinely complained about Pat being in their shorts.

"Well," I would retort, "that's what you get for being on the fun side of the business. No one wants to get into how the sausage is made on the HR side—it's not sexy enough, not when they could be looking at pretty pictures of coffee plantations." We would laugh, knowing on some level that this was true. I had found that most executives just wanted the people side of the business to work and didn't have much interest in what it took to get it there. And since I didn't grow up in HR, I had a much more intuitive style that allowed me to speak very practically about what we were doing to support the business.

If someone tried to tell me during that year that I was distracting myself with work, I would have pointed to a quote I had up high on the oversized whiteboard in my office: "Less talk, more action." I had zero tolerance for what I perceived as whining. I would not allow it in myself, which made it impossible to accept from others. Mine was an NWZ, a no whine zone.

I thought I could extend the NWZ to my home. I thought I could fix what was wrong by telling Daniel to snap out of it, stop complaining, just get with the happy family program. My radar for the truth was broken, switched off, and I willfully ignored very clear signs that impending danger was looming.

Toward the end of November, I made plans to go home for Thanksgiving to see my parents. When I arrived, I made some excuse as to why Daniel wasn't with us and tried to avoid my mother's eyes—or was she avoiding mine in the face of this flimsy lie of omission? If my mother suspected anything, she didn't say it. We followed our usual pattern, pretending everything was fine and speaking superficially about the logistics around the preparation of Thanksgiving dinner.

My mother's sister, Helen, invited us over for coffee, and as we settled into her home, whose decor dated from the 1970s, I was reminded how even as an adult it always felt like I had to walk on eggshells in my parents' home. Looking around her sunken living room, I remembered how when I was growing up, Aunt Helen's home had felt like a modern-day Sodom and Gomorrah. She had bright green shag carpeting throughout the house with beads hanging from doorways separating the living room from the den. She had a mirror with gold veins running through it above her bed. In the backyard was a hot tub with lush green plants that prevented the neighbors from witnessing the parties she hosted on a regular basis.

My Aunt Helen had bleached blonde hair, stood at just under five feet, and I'm sure didn't weigh more than a hundred pounds. She carried herself like Zsa Zsa Gabor, no matter her age, adding "darling" and "sweetheart" to the end of every sentence with her strong Lebanese accent. She also never mastered the art of compound words in English.

"Darling, please help me find my key car. I think I might have left them in the garage." Or "*Habibi*, Laila, please hand me my robe bath." As a child, I would giggle and correct her every time: "Car *key*, Aunt Helen." She would only smile and muss up my hair. "Yes, sweetheart, car key," she would repeat slowly, but then reverse the words immediately afterwards. My aunt had landed a job as a masseuse at the Dunes Hotel, and it wasn't long before she was running the spa there. Unlike our home, where my father's life outside of the home was a black box to me, my aunt's work followed her home. She always had people over, running in and out of the hot tub, sometimes with clothes on, sometimes not, laughing, eating, and drinking. Her two white poodles, Chi Chi and Baba, which she treated like spoiled children, ran freely in and out of the house and often wore knitted sweaters despite the Vegas heat.

"Darling, be careful with Chi Chi; he doesn't like it when you get too close to him."

My sister loved my aunt's home and soon spent most of her time there, but it scared the hell out of me, and I kept as far away from it as possible. I would take the scary place I understood rather than whatever this place was. The boundaryless nature of it left me wobbly. I needed more stability, security, so my visits became infrequent.

Driving my mother home with Nadia asleep in the car seat in the back, I had the urge to tell my mother everything, to fall apart and pour my heart out to her. The pressure inside me had risen to a point where I could barely keep it inside anymore, and I yearned to have a safe space to let it out, to be held and told it would be all right. But this was not our way. This would have required both of us to be more vulnerable, to be able to sift through messy emotions we had avoided our whole lives—a mountain of unspoken needs and desires mixed with unresolved disappointments. But mostly it would have required her to be strong for me, and we both knew implicitly that was not our arrangement. We kept our conversation light and breezy, staying on the surface, pretending everything was fine. I swallowed and tried to squelch the resentment that was rising within me. *Let it go,* I told myself. *Man up. You're fine.* This was my go-to place, both at work and at home. There was no woman better than me at manning up.

Daniel phoned to speak with Nadia on Thanksgiving night. Because Nadia was tired, she didn't want to stay on the phone very long, so after a few minutes she handed the phone back to me. I saw my mother watching this exchange, and I knew she could sense something was off. As I brought the phone to my ear, Daniel immediately flew into a rage, accusing me of turning Nadia against him, yelling at me uncontrollably. I tried to keep it together, unable to engage fully as I knew that my mother would hear me, but it didn't work. When I put the phone down, my mother asked me what was wrong, and I forced myself to look up into her eyes. I considered for a moment telling her everything, imagining I could collapse into her arms and release the fear that had been building up over the past few months, but I couldn't manage the disappointment of another failed conversation with her, so I kept it together emotionally and delivered just the facts.

"Daniel and I are separated," I finally admitted.

As expected, she nodded her head and walked out of the living room and into her bedroom. Not another word was said. If I had ever wondered where my ability to distract and deny had come from, here was my answer. I learned at the feet of the master.

———

I left Las Vegas a few days after Thanksgiving feeling sad and scared. Daniel really seemed to be spiraling to me, but I wasn't sure what I could do about it, or if I should do anything at all. I did nothing—I was so very good at doing nothing in my personal life. My fear numbed me into complacency at home, but at work it morphed into a ferocity that drove me to get things done. I was fearless at work, confident and competent in direct contrast to how terrified and inadequate I felt to engage in what was happening at home. As I went back to work, I subconsciously leaned into my head and clamped down on my heart, refocusing on what would be my first board presentation coming up in a few weeks. Pat had asked me to put together an overview on the work that my team had accomplished that first year and to lay out my HR strategy, which he wanted me to report on annually. *This,* I knew how to do, so I pivoted all my energy and focus back to work, cataloging all the things we had achieved that first year. I was excited to present my vision and long-term people strategy to the board, and I was grateful to have something important to distract me from my home life.

A week after Thanksgiving, as I was making Nadia dinner at home one night, Daniel asked if he could come over and bring Thai food. This was a rare moment of kindness I had not seen from him since he had moved out a couple of months earlier. I was worried he would become angry again, but I knew he wanted to see Nadia, so I agreed. It had been weeks since I'd seen him, and he looked like a ghost when he arrived on my doorstep. White and ashen, his normally full, heart-shaped face had become thinner and more angular. He was calm; I was relieved. I noticed he had scratches and scabs on his knuckles almost as if he had put his hand through a glass window.

"What happened here?" I asked, touching his knuckles lightly.

"Oh, nothing, I was working on my bike and scratched myself."

I don't know why, but I didn't believe him. He and I both knew there was a story around these scratches, but we both held up our part of our silent agreement: he, self-sabotaging, and me, pretending not to notice, both complicit in our silence. Later, I found out from his brother that he used to change the passcode on his devices while he was high and then not remember what they were later. He would end up getting so angry that he punched the device, breaking the glass and cutting himself in the process.

"Do you think I could stay over tonight?" he asked, looking down, avoiding my eyes. "I'm just so tired, and I'd rather not try to get home right now," he explained. "I can stay on the sofa if that's all right with you."

I agreed. We finished our pad Thai and chicken curry, the first normal interaction between us since he had moved out almost two months earlier. I picked up our dishes and took them to the kitchen sink, and when I returned to the sofa, I saw that he was already asleep. I touched his hair—his beautiful blond hair—and a chill went up my spine. I was so very sad for him, for us, for where we found ourselves. I allowed myself a brief moment to pause and felt a deep sadness start to make its way up within me, but before my eyes could fill with tears, I pushed it way deep down inside as if to move my hand away from a flame.

I passed a framed photo taken of us just a few months earlier at Nadia's end-of-the-year preschool art show. Nadia sitting between us, smiling and looking up in adoration at her daddy, my head leaning into his, his arm around my shoulder—a portrait of a young family at the start of their lives. I remembered a day at Children's Park where the Tickle Monster, aka Daddy, tried to catch Nadia as she ran and hid behind me but peered back over my shoulder to make sure he knew she wanted to be caught. Giggling, she dashed back and forth between us, collapsing into Daniel's arms as the Tickle Monster smothered her with kisses. I stared at his eyes in that picture for a long time, searching for the pain he must have been in, but I couldn't see a hint of it.

I turned away from the photo, turned off the lights, and walked toward my bedroom. Nadia was sleeping soundly in my bed, and I ran my fingers along her forehead as I walked over to close the bedroom door. As I turned the door handle, I paused, imagining he might wake up agitated, or worse. Would he storm into our, rather *my,* bedroom? Would he try to grab Nadia? I couldn't be sure. Frankly, I wasn't sure of anything anymore. I could only feel the tingling of the ever-present anxiety that was coursing through my veins. Quietly, I closed my bedroom door—and then locked it. Climbing into the bed next to Nadia, I felt a flash of guilt as I realized I no longer trusted the person who was on the other side of that door.

One week later, Daniel asked if he could spend the evening with Nadia while I went out. I agreed and felt it was safer to have him in our home rather than having her at his place, which was unknown to her, and me. I came home a few hours later to find the house in a complete mess. There was melted ice cream on the floor, clothes strewn everywhere. I made my way back to the bedrooms, my heart in my throat, terrified of what I might find, and there they were, both sleeping in my king-size bed. Daniel had a light on over him. His head was propped up on a pillow so that his whole face was enshrined in this golden light. He looked so peaceful that I hated waking him. It wasn't even ten o'clock. I breathed a sigh and touched him lightly. He awoke with a start and started pacing, immediately calling someone on his phone, making plans, and then he vanished. I don't even remember what we said to each other, he was in such a rush to leave.

The next night he phoned to talk to Nadia, and he felt very far away. He could barely speak, and he sounded very tired. We spent a few minutes on the phone and said goodbye. This was the evening of December 3. That was the last time we would speak to him.

The next morning, I dropped Nadia off at school, stopped by the Peet's at Laurel Village to pick up my morning cappuccino, and made my way to work. My presentation to the board was slated for the following day, and although I was excited about it, I was also nervous. I was making some final tweaks to the deck before meeting midday to review it with Pat. I knew I didn't have to worry about picking Nadia up because Daniel was on the schedule for that day, and he never missed pick-up. This was one way in which I could count on him.

My meeting with Pat was a little rocky—I felt unfocused and his critiques were sharp and pointed—and around four o'clock, my cell phone rang. I saw it was my daughter's school, so I excused myself from Pat, holding up a finger, and walked out of the room so I could speak. Calls about Nadia always took priority.

It was her preschool teacher on the line. "Your husband hasn't come to pick up your daughter," she said. My heart dropped. I wanted to tell her that we were recently estranged, that I had no idea where he was, that all I knew was that it was his day for pick-up, but instead I just told her I would send my nanny right away. It was for reasons just like this that I had made room in my home for a full-time nanny. I hung up and dialed Marci's number, trying to wipe away the feeling of dread that oozed through my veins and culminated in a thick, heavy puddle in the middle of my stomach. Ever since Daniel had left, I couldn't get rid of this feeling of trepidation. I prevented myself from thinking exactly what that might be, but this sudden disappearance tapped into something deep inside me I had been hiding from for months.

"Hey, Marci, it's me. Daniel didn't pick Nadia up today. Can you run over and pick her up please?" Marci agreed. I pressed "end" on the call and shook my head as a way to mentally wash away the strange feeling I had. *Nothing is wrong,* I told myself. *Nothing is wrong.* It was as if my body and heart were screaming at my head to pay attention to what was happening all around me, but my mind refused. Years of hiding had made me a master at avoidance.

A few hours later I sat at a trendy South Indian restaurant in the Mission with my girlfriends. These four women had become my closest friends over the fifteen years I had lived in San Francisco. On the face of it, each of us was very different, but the love and care we had for each other was undeniable and felt more like that of family than friends. We settled into our table and ordered samosas and drinks before we even looked at the menu. It was rare that the five of us could meet on a Tuesday night given our competing schedules of work, business travel, and kids' soccer games, and it felt nice to rest in the world-fusion vibe of the restaurant.

"How's it going with Daniel these days?" my girlfriend Karine asked gently as she leaned into me. Her son Rocky was born on the day that I found out I was pregnant with Nadia, which created a special bond between us. I hadn't really talked about our separation very much with my friends, only because I was still in denial myself. I had just told my mother the week earlier. Given this, I didn't fully express the fear that was rising inside of me as a result of Daniel's missed pick-up. Besides, I was also annoyed. How could he be so irresponsible?

"Okay, I guess," I answered. I tried to act nonplussed, denying the churn that had been swirling in my stomach. "The whole thing is just so weird. Ever since he moved out two months ago, communication has been very erratic, and today he was supposed to pick up Nadia from school and just never showed up. Didn't even call. That's just not like him, not when it comes to Nadia . . . I'm worried."

My girlfriends tried to reassure me that everything was all right, that Daniel could be a little flaky and that this wasn't completely out of character for him. I wanted to believe them, so I pushed down my worry while we finished dinner.

As I drove home that evening, however, a pang of fear pierced through the thin veneer I had managed to drape over my growing trepidation. I couldn't get past the fact that Daniel had never missed showing up for Nadia, no matter what. I tried phoning him several times but only got his voicemail. My mounting concern soon gave way to a low-grade feeling of uneasiness that I could not shake. I called and left a message: "Hey, are you there? I'm worried; I haven't heard from you, and you were supposed to pick up Nadia. Please call me. Let me know you're all right."

I went home to find that Marci had tucked Nadia in bed like always, and all was well. I convinced myself that whatever had happened with Daniel wasn't my problem. We were, after all, separated, and he wasn't my problem anymore.

I spent the majority of the next day at my first board meeting. Compared to the slides we looked at all day with financial statements and graphs, mine looked charming, or childish, depending on your perspective. I decided to use the hand-drawn illustrations from our Retail Operating Philosophy because they captured the spirit of the transformation we were working toward. Pat had laughed during our review, saying he was sure this would be the first time this group ever saw stick figures as part of a board presentation. I had felt so confident, but as I launched into my presentation, I was nervous as slide after slide showed hand drawings of stick figures representing different work tasks, one balancing another on his arm to show a balanced scorecard, another in front of a flip board to indicate training and development. I had built a pyramid with hand-drawn bricks with stick figures at each level representing each of my new leaders with their names etched underneath the drawing. I looked around the large, oval table and saw everyone smile, but I wasn't sure what was behind those smiles. At one point, Pat commented on one of the stick figures that had a big smile on her face and was holding up a coffee mug high in the air with a big P drawn on the front of the mug. This set off a chuckle in the room, and just as I thought I had gone too far with the drawings, the chairman of the board interjected that it was clear that a lot of work had been done and he appreciated the simplicity in how I was explaining what undoubtedly were complex problems to solve. I let out a big sigh. *Yes, he gets it.* That was all I needed to sail through the rest of my presentation with confidence.

Chatting with one of the board members after the meeting, I noticed I had no missed calls from Daniel, and as I got into my car late that afternoon, I tried him again but got no answer. On Thursday, I tried phoning him again, but this time his voicemail box was full. A pang of fear ran through me, but I refused to think the worst. *Denial, denial, denial*—next to distraction, it was one of the most powerful tools I had in my arsenal. Friday came, and I tried him again, but his mailbox was still full. My fear and anxiety began to bubble up. I started to panic, so I phoned his sister.

"Stephanie, have you heard from Daniel? I am worried. I haven't heard from him in a few days, and his mailbox was full. Could you please let me know if you reach him?"

She promised she would, but I didn't hear back from her. I told myself once again that Daniel was no longer my problem. I had alerted his family about my concern; what more could I do?

Sunday, Nadia and I went to a birthday party for the two-year-old daughter of a close friend at work. Walking with a juice box in one hand and a small paper plate with a slice of birthday cake in the other, I ushered Nadia to the kids' table and placed the treats in front of her. I rejoined a group of parents a few feet away, who were trying to have a conversation in between tending to their sugar-infused, hopped-up toddlers.

"How's Daniel?" one friend asked, and then another and another still. I struggled to find the right level of response for the question I had been obsessing over all week. I wanted to say, "I have no idea, and I'm sick with worry as I haven't heard from him in almost a week." But I kept it light, as was my style, more as a way to keep lying to myself that everything was all right than anything else. Having to answer questions about Daniel's whereabouts as I sat amongst intact families heightened my anxiety to the point where all I could hear was the beating of my heart in my ears, with muffled voices distant and garbled in the background. I didn't know what to think or do anymore. Daniel had left us, so there was a part of me that was trying to emotionally disconnect from him and get used to the idea that we were heading toward a divorce. At the same time, our separation had come on so suddenly and it was so new, so fresh, that my feelings for him were all tangled up inside. I was torn between trying to push him out of my consciousness so I could start moving on with my life and feeling like I needed to take care of him in the way I had been doing since first meeting him nine years earlier.

Eventually, I grabbed Nadia and left the party, starting the long drive from Menlo Park up to the city. I called Marci and told her I had to drop Nadia off. As I rounded the bend to get off the freeway on Fell Street, I began to cry. My body and my heart knew long before my head that something was seriously wrong. I could no longer ignore the sirens going off in my body. I was desperate to reach Daniel, to hear his voice, just to know he was all right. I didn't care if we were together. I just wanted to know he was safe. I looked in the rearview mirror and saw Nadia staring out the window in a trance, half asleep. Looking back, this was the moment my strong will and my denial were finally toppled over by what my heart and body knew. It was like a street fight, and my heart and body had finally gathered enough energy to stop the bully that was my head-based iron will. I was trying to protect myself by not allowing myself to feel. What I didn't know was that if you don't feel the pain, you can't be grateful for the love and goodness in your life. You cut off the lows, but you cut off the highs too, and all the nuances in between.

As if on autopilot, my mind no longer in control, I drove Nadia directly home so that Marci could get her ready for bed. Marci met me in the driveway to take Nadia upstairs. No words passed between us as our eyes met and she placed a gentle hand on my shoulder. "Don't worry about a thing here. I'll make the Bug a bubble bath and her favorite mac and cheese for dinner." Nadia laid her head on Marci's shoulder, her blonde locks intermingling with

Marci's black hair, and I was reminded of how grateful I was to have "Aunt Marci" in our life. I turned my car back to the closest police station, which happened to be in the Western Addition, one of the last few parts of town where there were projects and low-income housing. The short drive from my home to this part of town was like a metaphor for my shiny, perfect life colliding with the grittier truth screaming to emerge. There it was on display right before my eyes. The universe was yelling at me to wake up.

Getting out of my car, I took in the crisp December air, but I felt dizzy just the same. *Is this really happening? What am I doing?* I wanted to turn around and pretend everything was okay, but my feet continued to make their way to the square concrete building painted in seafoam green in front of me. I swung open the heavy door and stood inside a largely empty, dingy, open space that felt like a cross between an old public library and the Department of Motor Vehicles. There were corkboards covered with public-interest posters, and in the middle of the room was a counter that had bars and plastic separating me from the police officer sitting behind it. I approached and waited for him to look up at me. I didn't know where to start.

"Um," I stuttered, "I haven't heard from my husband in close to a week. I think something's wrong."

CHAPTER 4

THE DAM BREAKS

"The wound is where the light enters you."
—RUMI

The police officer blinked and stared at me blankly, waiting for me to continue.

"You see, he moved out of our house two months ago, and now I haven't heard from him in about a week." I could hear myself talking and saw that what I was saying was not communicating the sense of urgency I felt inside me. *He thinks I'm overreacting,* I thought to myself. *Am I overreacting? Oh please, God, let me be overreacting. I should just go, walk out and go home and forget this crazy idea.* Fear held me in place. "I'm worried because I know he has been, um, well, not behaving well, and I was wondering if you could send someone over to his apartment to see if he's all right?"

At this point, I was fighting back tears, and the officer spoke for the first time. "Ma'am, we can't go in if we don't have a search warrant."

"I see, but could you at least just knock on the door to see if he answers? It's not like him to just disappear like this."

"Well, why don't we check our databases to see if we can track him down?" This sounded promising, so I agreed.

"Where are you going to search?" I asked.

He answered while staring at his monitor. "I can search our own databases to see if he's been arrested, check the DMV to see if he's been involved in any accidents, the psych ward at SF General, and the morgue."

The morgue. There it was. My greatest fear spoken aloud. My stomach was in knots, and I couldn't swallow.

"Uh, okay," I whispered.

I was asked the make and model of Daniel's car and answered—a 2004 Volvo wagon. A few minutes later, the officer read off his screen without looking up at me: "It looks like he was involved in a hit and run. Just a minute, let me look to check our jail records." Hit and run? I felt dizzy but hopeful at the same time as this meant he could be alive, then the officer continued. "Wait, something's not right here. Remind me of your husband's name again?" I spoke it out loud again. A few minutes later, he said, "There seems to be two vehicles registered as a 2004 Volvo. This doesn't make sense." After twenty minutes of searching and calling for verification, the police officer explained: "It looks like your Volvo was mistakenly entered as a Volkswagen, and the VW was involved in a hit and run." My heart sank. That meant still no sign of Daniel. The officer continued his search and finally concluded that he wasn't registered at the jail, the psych ward, or the morgue. Daniel wasn't in the system.

"Would you like to file a missing person's report?" he asked.

My immediate feeling was that Daniel would not like this, and then I realized how ridiculous that thought was given the options presented. "Okay, yeah, but could you also please send someone to his apartment to check?"

This time, he radioed and dispatched two officers to Daniel's apartment. I was beginning to feel faint, my shoulders ached from hunching over the counter, and my legs tingled from standing for so long. I looked to see where I might sit, but all I saw were three low chairs with metal frames and stained fabric on the seats. I remained standing for what seemed a long time. The officer left the counter to do other things. I phoned my nanny to check on Nadia. I had been gone a couple of hours and it was getting near her bedtime, so I asked to say good night. Marci put Nadia on the phone, and hearing her sweet voice brought me out of my momentary nightmare but made the situation more real somehow. "Night night, my sweet girl," I said. "Mommy will be home very soon."

Thirty minutes or so passed, and the officer called me back to the counter. "Two officers knocked on your husband's door and called out. No one answered. As I said, we can't go in without a warrant."

But what if he can't *answer? What if he's there and he's hurt . . . or worse?* As if reading my mind, the officer offered, "Look, if he was in there and he was dead, they'd be able to smell something. A dead body gives off a strong odor." I didn't know what to say. I was having an out-of-body experience at this point. This was a comment made on *CSI*, not to someone like me in real life—my life. I looked into the officer's eyes, unable to speak, and saw not crassness but compassion. I realized that this comment was meant to comfort me. Unable to do anything else, I thanked the officer, took my little piece of paper that had the missing report ID number on it, and left.

That night I had a dream so vivid I remember it to this day. I dreamt that Daniel was packing for a long trip. His stepfather, Ron, was in the room with him, and they were amiably chatting as Daniel folded and put away clothes into a suitcase. He was happy, with a big smile on his face, and he was young. He was the Daniel I had met nine years earlier. I woke up in a panic and ran to the bathroom, feeling sick. I was shaking but knew what I had to do. I had a dentist appointment that morning, and since I didn't need to go into work right away, I had also made an appointment to work out with my trainer. I dressed for a workout, then calmly looked up the name and phone number of the apartment building where Daniel lived. I asked to speak with the manager and explained to her that I had not heard from my husband for a week, that officers went to his home yesterday evening but that there had been no answer, and could I please come over to make sure that everything was okay. She hesitated and responded that if I phoned the police again and gave them her name, she would let them into the apartment. I was relieved to not have to do this myself and agreed to her terms. I phoned the police station and explained to the officer on duty my situation, and he decided to send two officers to Daniel's apartment. My body was buzzing, and my ears were ringing. I felt myself backing away from the impending truth. I didn't know what to do, so I defaulted to my go-to place: distraction. *Just keep moving; you have no evidence that anything is wrong, so just keep forging ahead.*

I drove to the gym to meet my trainer, but during my workout my defenses began to weaken. I started to cry. My trainer tried to assure me that everything was all right and I nodded in agreement, but the tears continued to silently flow. I showered and changed for work, pulling my phone out of my bag as I left the gym, but there were no missed calls. I phoned the apartment manager and was told she was in a meeting. I hung up and called the police station, but the officer I spoke with could not be found. "Try back in a little bit," I was told. I felt lost. I wanted to scream. In the absence of any information, "nothing" was wrong, and yet everything in my body told me everything was wrong.

I went to my dentist appointment. While sitting in the chair, I remembered that Daniel was supposed to return to work the previous week, so I tracked down his boss's information and e-mailed to ask if Daniel had shown up. I nervously checked my phone each time the hygienist took her dental utensils out of my mouth. One new message from Daniel's boss appeared: "Hi, Laila, Daniel was supposed to come back on Tuesday the fourth, but he phoned on Tuesday morning to say he wasn't feeling well and that he would come in on Wednesday the fifth, but I haven't heard anything from him since then." *Oh God. Oh God.* My stomach churned; I felt sick. It was getting harder to convince myself that I was imagining things. I left the dentist's office and phoned the police station again, but there was no new information.

I didn't know what to do. Should I go home? Go to work? What would I do? I made my way to my car, and muscle memory kicked in. I did the thing I knew how to do well: I got on the Bay Bridge and began driving to work. I called the police station again, and the officer on the phone gave me another number to call and said something about a "medical examiner." I was in such a state of hyper-anxiety at this point that I didn't fully understand what was happening. In my mind, "medical" was good; Daniel must be at the hospital. I dialed the number.

"Hello. My name is Laila Tarraf. I was given your number by the Turk Street police station. They told me you might have some information on Daniel Forland?"

"Yes, could you please tell me your relation to him?"

"I'm his wife," I breathed, and heard my voice shaking. I began to silently cry.

"Could you please tell me if he has any tattoos on his body?"

"Yes," I sobbed. "An eagle on the left side of his back." I heard a sigh.

"I'm afraid I have the worst possible news . . ." he said, and his voice trailed off, not finishing his sentence.

As if a dam had broken, all the fear and anxiety I had been keeping bottled up flooded forward, and I heard myself say, "No, no, no, no . . ." I couldn't think of anything else to say. I banged the steering wheel with my hand. *No, please, God, not this. This is not happening.*

I tuned back into what the medical examiner was saying. "Ma'am, ma'am, where are you?"

"I'm on my way to work on the Bay Bridge," I managed to choke out.

"Ma'am. Please pull over and call me back when you are safe and stationary."

There is nowhere to pull over on the Bay Bridge, so, wracked with sobs, my nose running, my face hot and wet, I continued to cross the bridge, fighting the urge to break down and curl up into a little ball. Driving was the only thing keeping me from disappearing into my grief. When I arrived in the East Bay, I was lost. I didn't know what to do. The thought actually crossed my mind, *"Should I go to work?"* I phoned my director, Elizabeth, but got her voicemail. What to do? I instinctively called Pat.

"I won't be in today," I said. "Um, Daniel's gone. I just found out. I don't know what to do, but I just wanted to, um, let you know, that I, um . . . won't be coming in."

"Oh my God, Laila, go home and I will be right there."

While Pat and I had developed a good working relationship, he was not a personal friend and had never been to my home. His immediate reaction to help me was very unexpected, and as I was in a state of shock, all I could do was agree. I turned my car around and headed back toward the bridge back to San Francisco. My vision blurry with tears, my heart pounding, my ears ringing, I tried to replay what had just happened. *Daniel is dead. I'm going home, and my boss is coming over. The CEO of Peet's is coming over.* I moved into action and phoned my nanny.

"Marci," I sobbed, "Daniel's dead, and my boss is coming over to my house. Could you please just make sure the living room is straightened up?" I was out of control and officially out of my mind with grief. I needed to control something.

I phoned my best friend. "Anh," I screamed, "Daniel's gone, he's gone!"

"What? What are you saying? I can't understand you."

"Daniel is dead," I said. *Daniel is dead.*

"Okay, I'm coming over right now."

I sat at my dining room table, unable to focus. I saw Pat, my friend Anh, and Marci huddled and murmuring amongst themselves. At some point Pat left and came back. He had gone to the police station to retrieve Daniel's personal effects. I stared blankly at him. He handed me a small manila envelope containing Daniel's wallet, his driver's license inside it. There was a loose dollar bill in there too. This was what was left of Daniel. I looked down at his wallet and turned it over and over in my hand. Pat and Anh left as the light began to dim and Marci suggested she make me something to eat, but I refused. Marci picked Nadia up from school, made us dinner, and I went to bed at the same time as Nadia.

The following morning, I had an interview scheduled with the French American International School. Daniel and I had discussed sending Nadia to the French school because we both felt strongly about raising a bilingual global citizen. For me, it was a way to honor and stay close to my Francophile Lebanese roots, and Daniel was a French major in college—not because he loved languages but because he noticed that the girls in French class were much cuter than those in physics, so he switched majors. Despite our different backgrounds and reasoning, we had both spent time in Paris and wanted our daughter to be raised in an international, multilingual community; the school was a central part of our plan. As I got up that day, I forgot for an instant the nightmare I was in, but even as the previous day's events flooded into my conscious mind, I thought I could probably handle a short interview for kindergarten. I made a cup of Major D in my press pot and sat in my bay window staring at Sutro Tower and watching the sky get lighter and lighter. Soon, I heard footsteps on the stairs outside my door and a gentle knock on my door. I shuffled over to the door and let Marci in. She had two cups of coffee in her hands.

"Hi, honey, how are you?" she asked gently, handing me one of the cups.

"I'm fine, I guess. I just remembered I have that interview at French American. I need to start getting ready, I think."

Marci stared at me without a word.

"What?" I asked. I was so programmed to get work done, to complete my to-do list, to just keep moving no matter what I was feeling inside, that I couldn't fathom any other way.

"Laila, I think it would be better if you did that at a later time, don't you think? I'm sure they would be accommodating. Do you want me to help?"

"Oh, no, it's fine. I'll call them and see if postponing is possible." The thought had not crossed my mind to do this. Just then I heard Nadia's voice, and Marci indicated she would get her while I made the call. I walked into my bedroom and closed the door, dialing the school's number.

"Oh, hi, yes, my name is Laila Tarraf. I have an interview today with Andrew Brown, the admissions director, to discuss my daughter, Nadia, who is applying for Pre-K next fall. I was wondering if I might be able to postpone that meeting to another time . . ." I fumbled for what to say, not wanting to freak out the receptionist by blurting out that my husband had been found dead the day before, and as that thought came to mind, I began to cry. "Oh, I'm so sorry . . ." I dribbled, unable to pull myself together. Luckily for me, the person on the line had more sense than I did and quickly let me know that it was not a problem to postpone the meeting until February and not to worry about a thing. I thanked her and pushed "end" on the call. What had just happened?

The next three days were a blur. I couldn't take anything in. I was just going through the motions, looking at myself from the outside in. On the third day, Pat called to check in on me, and after hearing my voice said, "Oh good, you sound a little better. I was really worried about you these past couple of days."

"I'm fine," I uttered, with less conviction than I was aiming for. I had always been able to make things fine by pretending they weren't really happening. "I'm going to focus on planning the memorial, and I'll be back to work in two weeks."

"You'll let me know if you need anything, right? I will see you after the holidays."

The magnitude of the loss became very real for me when it came to telling Nadia. The cognitive dissonance that was growing inside me as I was internally trying to accept the fact Daniel was gone while externally pretending everything was fine got the better of me. I was standing over the kitchen counter gently encouraging Nadia to eat the veggies on her plate when all of a sudden, an overwhelming feeling come over me. I had to let her know; I simply couldn't keep it in any longer. It felt like this terrible truth was swimming all around us, and it began to feel dishonest to withhold this information from her. I didn't want to have the same kind of relationship with her that I had with my mother. So, I began:

"Nadia, honey, I need to tell you something." She continued picking at her food, not looking up. I looked up into my nanny's eyes, silently asking for her support, and Marci gently nodded, tears already brimming in her eyes. I leaned in a little closer to Nadia and said, "Something bad has happened to Daddy. He fell and hurt himself, and when you fall very badly and hurt your body very, very badly, then your body stops working, and this is what's called dead." My heart was beating loudly in my ears and I held my breath, anticipating her reaction. I had been advised to keep the explanation short and very tangible and concrete for someone of her age—that the abstract concepts of death were beyond the ability of a three-year-old to grasp. So, I tried to stay focused on what I thought happened physically to him. What made matters worse was that I didn't know exactly what had happened. All I knew at this point was that he was found dead on his bathroom floor.

She looked up, slowly processing this news, and turned to me and said, "What? Daddy's dead? What?"

"Yes," I responded. "He hurt himself very badly, and his body stopped working." It felt like I was whipping her with these words each time I repeated them—sharp, spiky, trauma-inducing words. I searched my brain for better words, for language that might soften the horror of the situation while at the same time conveying what had happened. I could see Marci out of the corner of my eye crying. Suddenly, Nadia became very animated and began to repeat my words, over and over again. Now I was the one being assaulted as my words continued to stream out of her mouth.

"Daddy died, he fell down and he hurt himself and his body stopped working? He fell down and his body stopped working? He's dead? Daddy's dead?"

"Yes, sweetheart, I'm so sorry," I repeated over and over, trying to hug her, but she was too agitated, so I just stayed close to her as she tried to process the unthinkable news that her father was gone. She started to cry, but she wouldn't stop repeating the words as if the more she said them, the better she would understand them. Over the following couple of hours, I tried to soothe her by drawing a warm bubble bath with lavender and chamomile, and I stayed with her as she played with her figurines in the tub. Eventually she forgot all about me and slipped right back into her normal princess play.

"Buggie, are you ready to get out?" I asked, looking at my watch and realizing it had been over forty minutes since she had gotten into the tub. "Bugs? Miss Nadia?" She was so engrossed in her play that I needed to kneel down and touch her on the shoulder for her to look up. "What do you think, lovey, want to get out? It's getting close to bedtime. If you like you can sleep with me tonight in the big bed."

She nodded her head enthusiastically and let a small smile emerge. As we lay in my king-size bed, Nadia settled into the crook of my arm and quickly fell asleep—safe and sound, I thought. Just then, I realized that I had the unenviable task of having to explain to her preschool teachers that Nadia's father had passed away. This thought made my stomach churn. What was I going to tell them? They had just seen Daniel a few weeks earlier. I didn't want to share with the school my suspicion that he had died of an accidental drug overdose for so many reasons. First, it was too intimate to share with practical strangers. Two, I worried that anything I told them would eventually leak down to Nadia, and I wanted to make sure I controlled the messaging to her until she was older and better able to understand the full extent of the story. But how else does one explain a young, healthy man dying suddenly?

The next day, after I dropped Nadia off at school, I sat in the preschool office across from Nadia's teacher and a school administrator trying to explain what had happened. They were kind and empathetic as I tried to stay as close to the facts as possible. They shared that Carly, another of the eleven children in Nadia's class, had also lost her father six months earlier after a long battle with brain cancer. In that moment, I wished that Daniel had died in a car accident or that he had lost his battle with cancer instead of with addiction. No one brings you casseroles when your husband is an addict. I heard some version of this quote many years later as more and more people were dying due to accidental overdoses, but these were early days, and I felt shame in wishing that Daniel could have died of something easier to explain to strangers. When someone dies at their own hand, accidently or not, a certain level of judgment is passed, and I wasn't sure to whom it was directed—toward Daniel, toward me, or even toward Nadia? The conversation was stilted, and I felt like they were waiting for me to share more information, but I continued to repeat the facts at a high level—that he had recently moved out, that he was found in his bathroom, that he had suffered a head wound and that we wouldn't know definitively what had happened until we received his toxicology report. Eventually, they stopped asking me questions and I thanked them for their time and left.

Over the next few days, Nadia's preschool teachers told me that Nadia continued to repeat the news that her father had died to anyone she came in contact with, "which as you can imagine is causing quite a stir amongst our other parents." Once again, the school was confronted with explaining the untimely death of another parent to a class of preschoolers.

Not surprisingly, Nadia and Carly developed a unique bond and spent the rest of the school year in a fantasy world of dress-up and make-believe together. Nadia stopped wearing pants altogether and more often than not donned not only a dress but a Disney princess gown for good measure. One day when I was getting ready to go to work, she emerged from deep within my closet and pulled down one of my dresses, handing it to me and saying, "Don't wear pants, Mommy. They are not beautiful." I scooped her up in my arms and promised that I would try to make a greater effort to wear more dresses. She signaled her approval with an enthusiastic round of applause.

Those first two weeks after we found Daniel were like living in a fog for me. The fact that they fell over Christmas and New Year's made sure I would have annual reminders of this loss. Though I wasn't going into the office, I received calls and e-mails every other day from my team members and other executives across the company. As word got out, people began to reach out with kind words and profound reminders of how much I was loved. My first lieutenant at work, Kristi, even made me CDs of beautiful songs and had them sent to my home with a heartfelt note telling me she was thinking about me. I turned my attention to the administration of death. It gave me something to do, and I was so very grateful for having these mundane details to focus upon.

I had avoided funerals as much as possible until this point in my life. In fact, I struggled with the concept of death in general, subtly avoiding attending the services of elderly relatives by opting to stay home with the younger kids or making any flimsy excuse that would get me out of going. Daniel used to tease me and say, "It's the circle of life, and you can't avoid death, Laila." I would plug my ears and playfully sing out loud, "La la la la la, I'm not listening!" We would laugh over this, and he would shake his head at me as if to say, *What am I going to do with you?* I couldn't—or wouldn't—even entertain the idea of any sort of suffering. *Happy happy, joy joy* was my life's mantra, and there was no room for pain in my world. Yes, it was true that I had to keep moving mentally, emotionally, and physically to avoid the inevitable hardships in life, but I was strong and capable, and it seemed a small price to pay for being able to avoid the messiness of life.

In the end, the irony was not lost on me that Daniel had become my greatest teacher in learning to accept death. Anh came to pick me up to go to a funeral home and make arrangements for Daniel's services. I sat, disoriented and numb, in a disheveled funeral home office perusing a binder that held a variety of prayer cards with comforting poems and sayings on them that, apparently, you were supposed to make available to mourners. My eyes scanned biblical quotes and simple poems set against photos of floral gardens, clouds and sunsets. There's a whole industry focused just on what needs to be said when someone dies, I learned. I had gone through most of the binder unable to find anything that captured our situation.

How did I get here? In three months—the same time it took me to create a powerful roadmap for a new culture at Peet's—my life had turned on a dime. In October Daniel had moved out of our home, by Thanksgiving he had served me with divorce papers, and by mid-December he was gone. Dead. I could hardly catch my breath, not only due to the series of these life-altering and improbable events but also due to the pace at which they had transpired. No sooner had I started getting my head around the fact that I might get divorced, I found myself a young widow with a toddler in tow. I suspected that my worst fear—the one I had never fully articulated to anyone, including myself—seemed to have materialized. This awful feeling that if I didn't keep a steady hand on making sure that Daniel stayed on the straight and narrow road, he would careen off into a ditch. But I couldn't be sure how he died, as I was told it would be months before the toxicology report would be complete. Scanning the binder, my eyes landed on a poem called "I'm Free." As I started reading it, my eyes filled with tears. *This is it, this is it,* I thought.

> *Don't grieve for me, for now I'm free*
> *I'm following the path God laid for me.*
> *I took His hand when I heard Him call;*
> *I turned my back and left it all.*

It ended with "God wanted me now, He set me free." The woman at the funeral home was kind, compassionate, and unexpectedly funny, smiling and making light-hearted small talk that lessened the heaviness of the task at hand. She grabbed several tissues and handed them to me, and as I gathered myself, I pointed to the poem I had chosen.

"Ah, yes, that's a good one. One of my favorites," she said, smiling kindly.

As she went through the administrative details and decisions I would have to make, my mind kept flashing back to episodes of *Six Feet Under*, wondering what Nate and David Fisher's lives were like having to deal with grieving people all day, every day. I couldn't accept the reality that this was really happening, so I kept mentally parachuting myself into scenes from all the countless TV shows I had ever watched. *CSI, Six Feet Under*—I grabbed anything that could offer me even a moment of mental escape. I wasn't ready to permanently land in this new reality of mine, so I kept my mind as busy as possible with details and daydreams. I honestly can't remember how I decided on cremation except for the fact that I thought Daniel wouldn't like to be locked up in a box. He needed to be free in death in a way that he could never attain in life, just like the poem said. I decided to do a closed-casket ceremony for close friends and family right away before Christmas and then a bigger celebration of life memorial after the holidays to allow more people an opportunity to attend and say goodbye. Daniel was a member of the St. Francis Yacht Club because he sang in their men's choir, and I thought he would have liked to have his ashes spread at sea with a memorial service at the club beforehand.

A week after Daniel was found, I held a closed-casket ceremony for family and close friends. I left Nadia at home with Marci and drove my mother, who had come to town the day before, to the funeral home. The Saint Francis Yacht Club Men's Chorus came and sang two very beautiful songs. The room was small, and I felt very alone. My mother chose a pew a few rows back and sat by herself in the middle. I didn't have the energy to go be with her, as I knew she was upset and needed comforting, but I didn't have anything in me to give. This had been a long-standing theme in our inverted relationship, but that day I couldn't go to her, and if I'm honest, I resented her for not being there for me. We were, the two of us, emotionally inadequate for the task at hand. Not knowing what to do with myself, I sat on the side of the room in a pew along the side wall. Midway through the ceremony, Daniel's brother, Scott, came over and sat next to me. It was so very unexpected, as Daniel's brother was a big, non-emotive Northern European type, and tears flowed silently as he took my hand.

After the ceremony was over I told everyone I would be out in a moment. Once they'd all left the room, I walked up to Daniel's coffin, put my hand on top of it, and allowed myself to truly sob for his loss. My chest was so constricted; it ached around my windpipe and rib cage. *Goodbye, Daniel. I'm so very sorry for, for . . .* What was I sorry for? I was just sorry. Sorry for the fact that I couldn't, or wouldn't, save him, sorry for the childhood he had suffered at the hands of a physically abusive stepfather and a mother who was unable to protect him, but mostly I was sorry for all the future events he would miss in not seeing his daughter grow up. I wished I could have seen him one last time. I replayed in my mind the last seconds of the last time I saw him, and even in that memory, I couldn't see his face. He was in a rush to leave, and I can only remember him answering a call, his back to me, his hair falling in his eyes as he walked out of the front door for the last time. I understood very personally in that moment the need for closure, the need to psychologically wrap something up and put it away. Without it, the pain is like a wound that won't heal, open to being reinjured every time another memory is triggered. It would be years before I dropped the ongoing dialogue in my head about how things could have played out differently.

A week later I flew home to spend Christmas with my family. I lay awake that first night, a few days before Christmas, in the spare bedroom of my parents' home, lonelier and more scared than I had ever been in my life. Since I had left home at eighteen, I was used to the weird feeling that came over me every time I came home to visit. *Am I the only person who experiences this?* I wondered. Each and every time I came home, I would feel like I'd regressed to the person I was before I left. No matter how much I had accomplished or evolved emotionally in my life, coming back home was like hitting the reset button, and all the old emotions and insecurities would come flooding back. I felt constrained and contained, unable to be who I had become, not just with my parents but with my brother and sister as well. My life felt too big to bring into this small container, so I had to make myself small too. This smallness extended to my emotional range as well; I slipped back into our dysfunctional familial patterns like a hand gliding into a glove—every groove, every ridge well-worn and well-trodden.

You know those stories you tell yourself your whole life? "When this happens, *then* I will get what I need or want or deserve." *The island where everything works out*, my coaching instructor later called it. Going back to Las Vegas for Christmas, after Daniel's death but before his celebration of life service, shattered a long-held belief of mine: the belief that when I needed my family to be there for me, to comfort me in my moment of suffering, they would step up. They would open their arms to hold me and comfort me so that I wouldn't have to be the strong one. I could finally put down my mantle and they would take care of me. This was how I justified small moments throughout my life where I yearned for a mother or father who could be more supportive of me. Not financially but emotionally. My mother and father had a very tumultuous relationship where they openly fought our whole lives, so very early on I got the sense that my parents were too engrossed in their own battles to be able to be there for me, to meet my needs emotionally. I tried to make myself very independent and show them that I didn't have many needs and that I didn't have to be an additional burden on their already strained relationship. I was the exact replica of Joy in the Disney movie *Inside Out*. When Joy draws a circle around Sadness and tells her to stay in that small space, I felt a deep shame because that is what I had been doing my whole life. My inner Joy didn't allow my inner Sadness more than a centimeter of space to express herself. I let Joy run the show and locked Sadness away.

But somewhere deep in my subconscious I never gave up hope that when I really, truly needed my parents, they would be there for me. In hindsight, this was not a very good strategy because as time went on, I became more and more self-sufficient, which made it more difficult for me to show or ask for any sort of help or attention. I just kept on pushing down my disappointment, one swallow at a time, until I actually forgot that I possessed the very basic need of wanting to be cared for by my parents—or anyone for that matter.

But this time, I couldn't convince myself any longer that this didn't warrant their love and attention. As I grappled with this realization, I heard voices out in the living room. I slowly made my way out there and saw that my father, who had recently suffered a stroke and who I thought was incapable of carrying on a conversation, was in full dialogue with a friend and was speaking quite eloquently about what had happened. He was relaying the story of Daniel's death to his friend but had not said a word to me since I had entered the house the day before. *What is this? He's able to converse on this level, but he couldn't speak with me?* It was as if I'd gotten punched in the solar plexus. I quickly went back to bed before he could see me, my head spinning with this new information, trying to justify his behavior with any sort of excuse so as not to face the obvious. I awoke the next morning to a day filled with awkward moments and welcome distractions in attending to the care and feeding of a young child. By the end of the evening, I was in so much emotional pain, my skin actually hurt. As I was getting Nadia ready for bed, my mother brushed by me and I couldn't hold back any longer.

"Mom, why aren't you talking to me? What's going on?" I finished pulling Nadia's nightie over her head, and she ran out of the bedroom back out to the family room. I got up off the floor and stood face-to-face with my mom. It felt awkward for me to confront her, as I had never asked my mom to be more present, because deep in my heart I think I always knew that she couldn't. Putting her on the spot in that moment meant it was D-Day. I held my breath waiting for her response.

To my utter disbelief, she jeered at me and said, "What? You don't think this hurts me too?" She turned her back and started to make her way further into the bedroom.

I was dumbfounded. For a moment, I didn't really understand her answer, and then, as if a dam broke, a flood of understanding washed over me. Even in this moment, in my absolute hour of need, it was not about me; it was about her. I hung my head and sunk into this truth that I had been weaving and bobbing to stay away from my whole life. Sadness turned to anguish, which turned to anger.

I reached out and turned her back by the shoulder to look at me. I wailed at her, "This . . . right here, right now, is NOT about you! It's about me! I need you to be there for me!" Immediately, I felt the neediness in this comment and quickly tried to minimize the request. "Just right now, not always, just today, just right now . . ." I trailed off, unable to think of anything else to say. I wanted to make her a deal: please just help me with this tiny little crisis of mine right now, and I'll never ask for anything else. It felt as if I were naked, standing there pleading to have her comfort me.

She shook her head and walked out of the bedroom and back into the family room. I could hear her ask Nadia if she was hungry, and the moment of truth between us vanished. That was it for me. I could no longer pretend this was "normal" behavior. A mother and father who had the capacity to emotionally support their daughter would have stepped up in that moment, and they didn't or couldn't. It didn't really matter anymore. I knew in that moment that waiting and hoping to receive more emotional support from them was a pipe dream, a fool's errand, and I was done contorting myself and making excuses for their inability to comfort me.

I left Las Vegas the following day, unable to withstand the loneliness of being physically surrounded by family yet feeling completely emotionally abandoned at the same time. I threw myself into organizing and producing Daniel's celebration of life memorial as a way to keep myself going. I was good at organizing things, producing, directing, and leading them. I reverted back to my highest skill, and the thought actually crossed my mind that it was too bad I didn't have the kind of resources I had at work to truly create something special. I moved into my left brain and could almost forget the mind-numbing loss as I immersed myself in the details of organizing the memorial, creating a program, ordering the photos, sending out e-mails, scheduling the talent. I was in my element. I was in control, and I held on to that tiny piece of certainty as if my life depended on it.

CHAPTER 5

WEATHERING THE STORM

"Daniel, you're a star in the face of the sky."
—ELTON JOHN

A fierce Pacific storm raged on the day we celebrated Daniel's life. Hurricane-force winds with torrential rains pelted us all day long. The storm was so severe that morning ferry services across the bay were canceled as docked boats rocked like rubber ducks in a bath. In the city, street signs were down, and huge trees crashed onto parked cars. The news reported five overturned vehicles, including fire trucks overturned on the highways, and eventually bridges were closed due to extreme weather. It was the worst storm in the twenty years I'd lived in San Francisco. I couldn't help but wonder if Daniel didn't have a hand in the weather that day. Was this his way of saying, "I didn't mean for this to happen"? Was he trying to communicate with us? Was he trying to say goodbye?

Over one hundred people gathered to pay their respects at the St. Francis Yacht Club, in a room overlooking the gray, choppy waters of the San Francisco bay. In the distance, Alcatraz Island provided a hazy backdrop to a landscape punished by wind and rain. Inside you could hear the howling of the wind and the heavy rain pelting the roof, and every time the door was opened, a cool draft swept in and blew through the room. There was a grand piano in front on the left side of the room where we had placed Daniel's ashes in a wooden urn carved with a picture of the Golden Gate Bridge. Next to it was a close-up of him and Nadia, taken just a few months before, and other framed pictures were placed throughout the room. A fire crackled in an oversized fireplace as Mike, the head of the men's chorus, stood up to greet everyone. The moment he began his welcome, logs fell, and sparks flew up as the fire roared to life. It was so dramatic and so perfectly timed that Mike held his arms up and said, "Yes, Daniel, we hear you and know that you are with us." A nervous laugh went up from the crowd, but it was very clear to me that this was Daniel making his presence known. To me, it felt as if he was just on the other side of that storm wanting to get back into our world.

I sat at a round table at the front of the room with Nadia in my lap and a few close friends and Daniel's family around me. No one from my family came to Daniel's celebration of life service. I didn't even really notice until months later when I was speaking with my therapist and relating the story of Daniel's service. He stopped me in my tracks to verify: "No one from your family attended the funeral of your husband?" When he said it that way, it felt like a hard slap in the face. I immediately recoiled from this truth, embarrassed. *What was wrong with me that I wasn't worth comforting in my hour of need?*

"Well . . ." I began to explain, making excuses for them all, "my mother had already attended the closed-casket ceremony, and my dad, well, you know, he's not been the same since he had his stroke, and my brother had to work, and, actually, I'm not sure about my sister . . ." He looked me in the eyes and said, "Imagine this was Nadia and she had lost her husband. Would there be anything that could stop you from going to her to be by her side to comfort her?" My eyes filled with tears. Of course, I would be there for her. I would move heaven and earth to try to soothe her pain.

I had become so accustomed to going it alone, to not relying on anyone that I didn't even notice when my own family didn't step up to help me in my darkest moment. The insidious thing about this story I had told myself was that it also prevented me from seeing when people were available and willing to help. I mentioned to one friend at the beginning of the service that I couldn't believe how many people had come to say goodbye to Daniel, that I didn't realize how much these people had cared for him. She looked me straight in the eye, delicately touched my arm, and said, "Laila, these people are here for you, honey. We care about you, and we're all here to support you."

"Oh," I replied, this obvious fact so lost on me, it knocked me a bit off-center.

For weeks before the ceremony, I tried to think of who could deliver the eulogy on my behalf. I didn't want to do it. The pain was too much. It was too personal, too intimate to stand up in front of our closest friends and family and authentically speak about my estranged husband's passing in front of everyone I knew. But even as I tried to find a way out of it, I worked on the speech, trying to find the right words that could capture and make sense of the situation and a cacophony of divergent feelings.

My mind often circled back to the moment we met. I was at a house party off Union Street waiting for the bartender to make my drink. The year was 1998. I had just moved back from Paris, and my newfound French style had not yet given way to the standard San Francisco uniform of jeans and black boots. Wearing my brown suede-in-the-front, spandex-in-the back pants paired with a light, tight-fitting tank top, I felt slightly more elegant than the other guests. I grabbed my Absolut vodka tonic from the bartender, and as I was stirring my swizzle stick, I looked up and saw Daniel walk into the room. He was beautiful with his gorgeous blond hair, warm brown eyes, and big bright smile. He was almost floating through the crowd, and all of a sudden he was standing in front of me. I stepped back in embarrassment, as I hadn't meant to be so obvious.

"Hi, I'm Daniel," he said. He held out his hand and immediately moved into my personal space with a familiarity that made me wonder if I had met him before, but when I asked, he said, "I'm Norwegian," as if this explained it. I gave him my number before the end of the night, and he phoned me a few days later and asked if I'd like to see the new Warren Miller movie at the Palace of Fine Arts. *The Norwegian wants to see an adventure ski film.* I smiled to myself. *Sounds appropriate.*

I enjoyed being with Daniel, but it was hard for me to take him seriously. For one, he was over ten years younger than me, but also he just had a boy's energy—a boy who grew up in the country. He was a maker. I was a city girl; I bought things I wanted. He was always tinkering with things trying to figure out how they worked so he could make them himself and make them better. He parked his car wherever he found an open spot and accumulated parking tickets like coupons.

"This is a city, Daniel," I used to remind him. "There are rules around parking, and you have to be careful. You can't just park your proverbial pickup truck on the side of the road here." We'd laugh about this, but he continued to do it.

I dated Daniel on and off for over a year, never committing to the relationship fully because of our age difference and because it was clear to me he was still very much in the party phase of his life. I didn't recognize in the beginning that his partying was an indication of deeper problems with drugs and alcohol. One day as we sat on my sofa in my Marina apartment, he asked me once again to give him a full commitment.

"You really think you're ready?" I asked.

"Yes, I really am. I've been telling you for a while now."

"Okay, let me be specific about what that entails," I said, and began to rattle off a list of my expectations, as if I were interviewing a candidate for an important position at work. "I want to get married; I want to have children; I need for you to be responsible and stable . . ." I went on and on, half expecting him to cry uncle, but he just sat there with this bemused smile on his face. Finally, I took a breath. "Do you think you can do all that?" I asked.

He looked me straight in the eye and said, "Well, not all of it right now, but I'm sure I can get there. I mean, I really want to."

Any rational person could have told you the gap between us was too large to bridge. If I really had been interviewing a candidate for a job, I would have dispassionately turned him down, noting the apparent "skill" gap between the job specification and his level of experience. But in my personal life, I wasn't thinking clearly. I was emotionally snagged, and as we both wanted it so badly—even if we didn't fully understand why at that point—we convinced each other it would all turn out all right.

"Okay," I said, "you've got yourself a commitment."

I could never have foreseen that the commitment we made that day could have set off a series of events that would land me at the St. Francis Yacht Club preparing to give Daniel's eulogy, but that is exactly what transpired. In the end, I knew no one else could deliver that eulogy but me. I lifted Nadia off my lap and handed her to my friend Carolyn, who was seated next to me. I walked to the front of the room unable to look up and really take in everyone around me. *I just need to read the words on the page,* I said to myself. *Just get through this and then you can sit down.* My heart was pounding so loudly I couldn't hear anything else. *I don't want to do this; please, God, help me.* Slowly, I opened the folded paper, looked up, and began:

"Thank you all for coming today. I am touched by how many people have reached out to show their support to Nadia and me over the past few weeks. I am grateful for your love, generosity, and friendship, and I am certain that Daniel would be pleased to see how many people he has touched throughout his all-too-brief life. I've written a few words here about Daniel that I would like to share with you today." I unfolded the pages in my hand and smoothed them out on the pedestal. My hands were shaking, my throat dry, my heart beating fast. The fleeting thought that I was simultaneously handling two of life's most stressful situations—death and public speaking—passed through my mind. As I made my way through the eulogy I had written with the help of my friend Dana—the first of many, I would soon realize—I noticed that people were responding to what I had written, and I started to relax a little. *This isn't so bad. I can do this.*

I paused, took a breath, and looked up. My eyes caught Nadia's, and she immediately jumped off Carolyn's lap and walked straight up to me at the front of the room. She was so small, barely twenty-five pounds. I put my hand around her shoulders and tried to continue, but she continued to hold her arms up to me, so I bent down and picked her up and set her on one hip. I continued:

"Nadia and her father became partners in crime. Always young at heart, Daniel found the curiosity of his little daughter the perfect match for exploring the world together . . ."

Nadia put her head on my shoulder and began to stroke my hair. This gesture was so loving and kind, it almost brought me to my knees. She was trying to comfort me. My baby girl could do what no one else in my family was able to do. This realization was almost too much for me in that moment. I paused and shifted my weight to hold her higher on my hip. She was getting heavy.

"I often called Daniel 'shiny.' He walked into a room and his presence was immediately felt. It wasn't just that Daniel was attractive, which he was. It was that for the things that he cared about, there was no middle ground. The way he dressed, the way he did his hair, even his skincare products, all reflected Daniel's desire for the world, including himself, to be as beautiful as possible."

I know a thing or two about hiding my pain too. This thought made me begin to sob.

Keep it together. You're almost there. Nadia hugged me tighter. Tears flowed silently as I willed myself to go on. Nadia gazed at me lovingly and provided me with the strength to continue. Even in this moment of gut-wrenching grief, I noticed how she was able to stay fully present with my suffering. I marveled at this angel of God.

Choking, I concluded. "Daniel, we wish that you are among the beauty and perfection that you sought in life. We hope that whatever it was that you were looking for, you have found. But most importantly, we hope more than anything that you know we loved you, will always love you, and will miss you." At this Nadia smiled, and I nearly collapsed as I set her on the ground and made my way back to my seat. *No more, please no more.*

Daniel's sister, Stephanie, a singer-songwriter, approached the front of the room and began to play the Elton John song "Daniel" on the piano. Her voice was so beautiful, and I had never before realized how perfectly the words captured the moment: "Daniel, my brother, you are older than me. Do you still feel the pain of the scars that won't heal? Your eyes are dry, but you see more than I. Daniel, you're the star, you dazzle the sky . . ." Daniel was indeed her older brother and had suffered at the hands of their abusive father and was now free to see more than she. *How could this be?* I thought to myself. I had chosen this song because it held Daniel's namesake, but I had never really anchored into the words. Each word, each phrase pierced my heart as I took in the unexpected yet almost perfect parallels between a song written years ago to what we were all experiencing today.

Afterwards, Stephanie sang an original composition she wrote for Daniel called "Stay with Me." As the melody settled over the room and Stephanie's clear, deep voice carried us all into this in-between state, lost in our thoughts, our pain, our reflections of our own lives, Nadia all of a sudden jumped off my lap and picked up the framed picture of her and her father that was sitting on top of the piano. She began to dance with it in the front of the room in front of everyone. I watched her as she twirled in her dress, solely focused on the framed picture of her and her daddy in her hands. She was completely unaware of anyone else in the room. I was in awe—dumbfounded—unable to do anything but follow her delicate movements as she waltzed across the front of the room. Someone next to me squeezed my hand, which brought me out of my trance. I looked up and noticed everyone in the room frozen in time, transfixed on the scene in front of them. I saw my anguish reflected in each and every person's eyes and felt a bond with them in that moment that I knew would last a lifetime. Scanning the room, I saw grown men—my boss, my business school friends, husbands of dear friends—all barely standing under the weight of the moment, not a dry eye in the house. And in the midst of the concentrated pain of the moment, it seemed that we were all also brought together in a collective state of wonder, gazing upon Nadia and marveling, "Who is this angel who has the courage, the strength, and the purity to be in the moment and dance with her daddy for the last time?"

As Stephanie's song came to an end—"With eyes wide open, we're only vessels of flesh and bone . . . the golden ship has sailed on . . . we're finally home"—I looked around the room and saw red-rimmed eyes and tears flowing everywhere. For the first time that day, I looked deep into the eyes of the people who were there: all my friends, my work colleagues, a few people I didn't know from Daniel's work. We were all motionless and united in the weight of that moment.

It would stay with me throughout my life.

The storm receded the next day and left in its wake a gray, blustery day. Leaves whipped and scattered outside, and inside everyone began to scatter back to their homes as well. There I was for the first time since this whole unimaginable nightmare began: it was just Nadia and me. "Just us now, baby girl," I whispered. We spent most of that Sunday in our pajamas shuffling around the house, climbing in and out of bed, clinging to each other. I couldn't wait for morning, when I could wrap up all my emotions into a neat little package and put it away, so I could go to work and do what I knew how to do.

CHAPTER 6

A PARTICULARLY TOUGH CASE

"And now here is my secret, a very simple secret:
It is only with the heart that one can see rightly;
what is essential is invisible to the eye."
—THE LITTLE PRINCE

Monday morning came, and I got up, took a shower, put on my work clothes, dropped Nadia at preschool, and went to work. Sitting at my desk, I absentmindedly scanned my calendar and noticed that I had an unaccepted meeting invite in my calendar for January 11, my birthday. It was from Daniel, and the subject line read "birthday celebration at Gary Danko." Daniel had made dinner reservations at our favorite restaurant for my birthday. I held my breath. I felt nauseous, and my muscles went weak. I lingered over his name in the "sent" field. How? When? My mouth was as dry as a drought-stricken field. My mind whirred trying to make sense of it all. I couldn't process it.

When I could breathe again, I called Gary Danko to confirm the reservation and asked when it had been made, but they couldn't tell me. How long had that invitation been on my calendar? There was no way to know if this was an invitation that had been put on my calendar a year in advance or a month in advance, but it was there, and it comforted me on some level that Daniel felt enough for me that he'd made that reservation as a surprise for my birthday, regardless of when he might have done it.

The next day, I got up and did the same thing, like the good little soldier I was. I made a cup of Major D's, Peet's signature blend, woke my baby girl, and got her ready for the short drive to her preschool before I turned my car to head over the Bay Bridge to go to work.

"Mommy, yesterday Carly and I dressed like princesses, all day long. I wore the pink Aurora dress and Carly wore the yellow Cinderella dress, and today I think we will switch." I half listened to her story as I cut up a few strawberries and put them on a pink plastic plate in front of her that was divided into three parts. I watched her organize her strawberries, cereal, and apple slices into each section.

"Oh, that sounds fun . . ." I interjected here and there, not fully following the stream of consciousness rambling of a three-year-old, yet grateful at the same time for the distraction. *Distraction, always my friend.* I glanced at the microwave clock and saw it was time to leave.

"You ready to brush your teeth so we can head out, Baby Bug?" I started putting the dishes in the sink and went to help Nadia climb down the elevated barstool she was sitting on.

"I can do it, Mommy," she muttered as she crawled down and ran to the bathroom.

"Of course, I keep forgetting what a big girl you are." I smiled at her and saw the pride in her eyes. *Don't grow up too fast on me.*

After a big hug at her school and a brief chat with her teacher about the previous day's events, I made my way across the city to the bridge. Work-wise, things were getting busy, which was just what I needed to give my mind something to focus on. I had recently gotten the go-ahead to build out the organizational capacity needed to support our expanding business. In fact, it was one of the top three priorities for the entire company and was foundational to the other two strategic imperatives, which were to strengthen retail stores and to expand our consumer business, which was our wholesale and grocery channel. My team took over the annual business kick-off meeting where we brought in our regional and district managers from across the country. For the first time since I had started at Peet's a year ago, I had a fully functioning team, and it felt good to come together and gel.

With my team's help, I was able to work through the summer, but eventually found that I was losing my stamina. I started making my way out to my car earlier and earlier every day, unable to work much later than four o'clock. I was a tangled knot of feelings: irritated, restless, sad, despondent, lonely, guarded, and yet indifferent to them all and to life in general. In one sixty-minute meeting, I could travel the range of these emotions, vacillating from being irritated by what I judged to be a ridiculous comment to feeling restless and bored in that same meeting, unable to concentrate on any details at all. There were moments I felt lonely and wanted the company of others and other times where I couldn't care less if I ever spoke with another human ever again because, after all, *what did it matter? We were all going to die eventually anyway, so what were we all getting worked up about?* I felt like a helium balloon that had lost its air, unable to soar to the heights I once did. Finally, I called my therapist, whom I had seen ten years earlier, to help me sort through my feelings.

Dr. Okin was a master in his field, and we had done deep work during the years before I found Daniel, when I was struggling with my decision to marry my then-fiancé, Terry. I was referred to Dr. Okin by a man named Tom and his wife whom we had met in Italy while I was on vacation with Terry. The four of us had been hiking back along the Via dell'Amore, the Way of Love, a path overlooking the Italian seaside linking the villages of Riomaggiore and Manarola in Cinque Terre, and had struck up a conversation. Tom and his wife were from Los Angeles and on their honeymoon.

Tom was also a recruiter like me, so we had a lot in common. As the day went on, they invited us to have dinner together. Here we were, two couples who had met only hours earlier, but as one does when meeting people on vacation or in transit, we developed an intimacy more easily than when at home. There's a sort of safety in the anonymity of it all—*or is that just me?* By the end of the evening, Terry and I had shared that we had been engaged for two years but that I was having a difficult time setting and committing to a date. I made light of this dilemma, certain I was being witty and charming, keeping the conversation light and lively, only mildly aware of the sideways glances Tom and his wife gave each other. After dinner, we joined others along the seaside path to take part in the Italian ritual after dinner evening stroll—*la passeggiata.*

Tom caught up with me, leaned in, and said, "You two have quite a story. Must be a difficult time for you."

"Oh, well, you know, I'm sure we'll figure it out." I was trying to keep it light, but he persisted.

"Laila, I just met you, but I feel I need to say something." My heart started to pound. "Look, I get it, you're smart, you talk fast, you're charming, and I bet no one calls you on your shit."

I thought I had misheard him. "What did you say?" I asked, genuinely trying to understand what he said.

"You heard me," he repeated. "I get it, you don't want to talk about it, and you're very good at staying away from what you don't want to talk about, that much is clear. But trust me when I tell you, this path will not lead to happiness for you. You need to go talk to somebody who can call you on your shit and help you figure some things out in your life."

I was dumbfounded. Who the hell did this guy think he was? And yet. There were sirens going off in my body, and a fear arose from deep within me. *Shit*, I thought. He had *seen* me. The real me—not the facade I was putting up—and I was scared. Just for an instant, I allowed myself to feel the longing to be seen, but the feeling was too raw for me to stay with, so I quickly pushed it down, breathing through the mild constriction in my chest. Instead, I tried to play it cool and replied with, "I'm sure I have no idea what you're talking about." I tried to sound unconcerned, but I'm sure my face betrayed me because it felt hot and exposed.

"Okay," he said, "but I want you to call my therapist in Los Angeles and maybe he can refer you to someone in San Francisco." I agreed if only to stop him from his verbal assault. Just then, his wife and Terry caught up to us and our brief, intimate exchange disappeared. My body was buzzing, my ears ringing, and I couldn't tune in to the conversation around me for the rest of our walk. As we returned to the restaurant, Tom handed me a small folded piece of paper with his therapist's number on it and we said our goodbyes. Terry smiled and turned his head sideways as if to ask, "What's this?"

"Tell you later," I whispered, not sure what I would say to him as I had never been honest with him about my doubts and I knew it was time to get real and make a decision.

We returned to San Francisco—and of course, dove back deep into my work. Each night I would come home, and Terry would try to advance the planning of our wedding. The more I resisted, the more he began to hold my feet to the fire about setting a date. Try as I might, I couldn't do it and I couldn't explain why. Every time we began to discuss details of our wedding day, a fear engulfed me, and I became paralyzed. One day, Terry walked into our living room and gently declared, "Listen, I'm not sure why this is so hard for you. I feel like I've been very patient, but I don't think I can wait any longer. I love you and I want to be with you, but if you can't make up your mind, then something is wrong here."

I couldn't say anything. I nodded, unable to disagree with him. I looked down at my beautiful engagement ring that I had been wearing for two years and pulled it off my finger, handing it back to him.

He looked down at the ring for a long time, turning it over in his hands. When he looked up, he had tears in his eyes but a smile on his face. "It's yours, whenever you want it back."

I nodded again, unable to speak, my heart in my throat. He pulled me close, and we cried silently together for the end of our relationship.

I didn't call the therapist's number right away. I was in denial. Sure, I was thirty-two years old and I had just broken up with my second serious boyfriend of three years, but I was still trying to convince myself it was them, not me. It took until close to Christmas before the soft faraway voice inside me grew loud enough for me to hear it:

"Call the damn therapist. You are not okay," it said.

"Fine," I retorted, *"I will call the damn therapist."*

Tom's therapist was kind when I phoned and explained my situation. He told me there were not many people who practiced this particular type of therapy but that there was one in San Francisco who was very good if I could get in to see him: Dr. Robert Okin.

I tried to get in to see Dr. Okin for months, but he was too busy. He referred me to a couple of other therapists instead. I tried both of them for one session each but determined quickly they were not going to be able to "call me on my shit." I was torn. I wanted to hide from them, to elude them, to distract them from the truth, but at the same time, I wanted them to catch me and help me figure out why I couldn't make a commitment, even if that thought paralyzed me with fear. Eventually, I called Dr. Okin back and threw myself at his mercy.

"Please, Dr. Okin, they can't do it. I think I'm a particularly tough case," I joked, unable to stay serious, "but I promise, if you see me, I will work hard." He finally acquiesced and agreed to see me. I had no idea what I had just signed up for.

A week later, I made my way to the seventh floor of San Francisco General Hospital, a large cluster of red brick buildings on Potrero Hill. SFGH was a trauma hospital serving the elderly and poor and held the largest acute inpatient and rehabilitation hospital for psychiatric patients in the San Francisco area. Dr. Okin, as it turned out, was the chief of psychiatry, and his office was at the end of a long corridor that required me to pass through the psych ward and an enclosed open courtyard each time I had an appointment with him. I became mesmerized by these patients, feeling into our common humanity each and every time I passed them.

On the day of my first appointment, I sat in a chair at the end of the corridor, fidgeting with my nails, waiting to be called into Dr. Okin's office. The door opened, and at first, I could only see an outline of him because he was backlit by the window behind him. As he moved closer to me to say hello, I felt his calm strength. He wore a cardigan and had ice-blue eyes with bushy eyebrows, giving him a wise professorial look. He smiled and shook my hand as he invited me into his office. His stillness made me nervous. I needed something to react to and he wasn't giving me anything, so I smiled, a small nervous laugh inadvertently spilling out of my mouth.

He looked me straight in the eyes and asked, "Is something funny?" My heart started to pound harder.

"Well, uh," I began, "I'm just about to share my most intimate thoughts and feelings with a complete stranger." I smiled and giggled again. He did not.

"And that's funny to you?" He stared right into my eyes, and I felt my face get hot.

Oh shit, I thought. *I've met my match.* I knew I could not dance around him and expect him to follow me. I sank into my chair, a knot in my stomach, feeling completely conflicted. I felt like I wanted to run out of the room as much as I wanted to stay and be caught. *"Catch me, please; I want to know why I can't make a commitment to save my life"* sat right next to *"Batten down the hatches; there's a storm coming in. Protect yourself."* In the one year I saw Dr. Okin, I held those two dualities in each and every session, simultaneously grateful for the progress we were making and yet terrified each step of the way that opening up somehow would weaken me, and then what? How would I manage?

I saw Dr. Okin three times in the first week alone for three to four hours each session. By the end of the week, I felt like a bloodied boxer, getting pummeled round after round. I started strong, giving him an overview of my early childhood.

"Well, my mom and dad didn't have a very good relationship, so I think that probably has something to do with my inability to commit to a long-term relationship," I rationalized to him, as if we were peers discussing an article we had read.

"How did that make you feel?" he replied.

"What? My parents' relationship or my inability to commit?"

"Tell me more about what it was like for you when you were young and your parents were fighting." It felt like he was inching closer to the things I did not want to discuss. "Can you share what some of your earliest memories were?"

My mind flashed to me pushing the Moroccan poof in between my parents, but I shook the image away. No way was I going to share that scene. Too honest, too soon, too much.

"What just happened?" Dr. Okin asked, leaning in a little closer.

"What do you mean?" I asked, genuinely confused.

"I just saw something in your face when I asked that question. Did something come to mind?" Closer and closer he came.

I looked down at my hands and tried to push the tears that were coming up as I thought about myself as a young girl trying to break up a physical fight between my parents.

"Um, well, yes . . ." I stammered, refusing to look up but unable to speak for fear I couldn't contain the emotion that was coming up inside me like lava threatening to break the surface of a volcano.

"I can see it's upsetting to you." He would not let it go.

No, no, no, keep it together, Laila. Don't fall apart.

But I could not wait him out. He just sat there looking at me, his blue eyes piercing a hole through my weakening facade. I felt emotionally exposed and disoriented. This was new territory for me. Hard as I tried, I could not push down my tears any longer, and without warning I unwillingly released years and years of sadness and pain that had been locked inside. The tight constraint around my inner Sadness had shattered, and she had a lot to say.

At first, I was annoyed and scolded myself, which only served to stall my therapy. My inner Joy had turned into the voice of a mean army general: *For God's sake, Laila, that's enough crying now. Seriously? What a fucking baby you are. There are people in the world suffering from real problems. What do you have to cry about? Get yourself together and get back out there, you wimpy piece of shit. Tell this guy to take a hike. You're fine, and all this crying is nothing but self-indulgent bullshit.* So, in addition to sadness, shame came along for the ride, but I kept going back, week after week, intuitively knowing there were no shortcuts, as much as I wished for them.

I had to work hard to arrive at a deeper awareness of my behaviors and my conditioned belief system; harder still to allow myself to feel the pain tied to those forgotten memories. Dr. Okin was not one to freely hand out pearls of wisdom that had not been hard-won. One such lesson was that you could not have safety and life at the same time.

"How do you feel about me?" he asked one session out of the blue.

"What do you mean? I'm grateful to have you in my life. I'm learning so much. I think we're making a lot of progress, don't you?" *What's he getting at here?*

"Yes, but how do you *feel* about me?"

Here we go, I thought.

He waited patiently as I drew a deep breath and really tried to go deep to tap into my true feelings. Not something superficial but something real and true.

"Well, sometimes I wish you were my father, and sometimes I wish you were my boyfriend." These words spilled out before I was fully aware of what I was saying. Immediately, I wished I could reel them back in. *Too much, too honest, too raw,* I thought. This admission was huge for me, and while I hoped he would let it go, I knew better and buckled up for the ride.

"Really? What would it look like if I were your father?"

"What?" The question threw me at first. "You know . . ."

"No, I don't really know what it means to you. Explain it to me."

"Well, you're someone I could go to for advice, and you're wise and you care about me and about helping me." I paused, hoping this would be enough.

I smiled and waited for Dr. Okin to ask me another question. He smiled back.

"More?" I asked. He only smiled. "Okay, well, you're also kind and supportive, and when I make a mistake, you're there for me and you love me anyway."

He nodded and waited for more. I searched my mind for what else I wanted from my father, but nothing concrete came to mind.

"I suppose it really comes down to feeling like he loved me."

"How does it feel to say these things to me?" he probed.

"It's a little embarrassing," I admitted.

"Why embarrassing?"

"Because it sounds so needy, I guess."

"It's embarrassing to need your father?" Dr. Okin gently asked.

"Yes . . . I mean no. I mean . . . I don't know." *Huh. Why was it embarrassing to express my needs and desires from my father?* "Maybe not embarrassing but a little uneasy. I feel nervous to just put these out there."

"Why?"

I knew why, but I didn't want to say. "I don't know." I sank into my chair and tried to wait him out. I didn't want to say it. I didn't want to say that I was worried he couldn't meet my needs, so I didn't want to put him on the spot. I knew that would sound ridiculous if I said it out loud, so I sat still, looking down.

We sat in silence, his gaze feeling heavy upon me. I became very engaged in the hem of my sleeve, trying to disappear into my chair. "This is embarrassing," I finally said.

"What is?"

"I'm embarrassed about being nervous to want my father to take care of me."

"Are you worried that he won't?"

A PARTICULARLY TOUGH CASE

Hell yes, I was worried. I was terrified because that's what my experience had been with him growing up. We were always tip-toeing around the house so as not to get in his way. So yes, I was fairly certain that my needs did not even make it into his top ten list of things he thought about. My strategy with my dad was to be invisible—to minimize my needs and myself so that I wouldn't inadvertently trigger his rage.

"Describe to me the kind of father I would be then for you," Dr. Okin continued.

Where do I start? I thought. I started to think about all the things I wanted my dad to be, but none of them seemed big enough to highlight as "Yes, this is the thing that I want," but as I played through the possibilities, I started to cry. I realized that really, all I wanted was for him to care *about* me, not necessarily care *for* me. I just wanted him to love me.

Dr. Okin let me cry for a long time then he smiled and said, "Good." I could not see what was good about my dissolving into tears in that moment and he must have seen the confusion on my face.

"Now, can you tell me what it would look like if I were your boyfriend?"

My boyfriend? Nothing. Nothing came to mind—a blank slate. I couldn't even think of going there. It felt weird to imagine Dr. Okin as my boyfriend, especially since he was sitting right in front of me. I sat in silence for a long time.

"Laila, can you tell me how it would be if I were your boyfriend?" he persisted.

"Uh, well, you know, you would be kind, and loving, and considerate . . ." I knew that my answers were stilted, but I was afraid to allow myself to *feel* what it would be like for him—or anyone—to be my boyfriend, so I stayed on the surface. I stayed in my head.

"How would that feel?" He tried once more to go deeper.

"Uh, it would feel . . . good. You know, um, yes, it would feel good." I looked up at the clock behind Dr. Okin and saw we only had a few minutes left in our session, so I stayed on the surface and slyly let the clock run out.

Finally, Dr. Okin sighed and handed me a present, saying, "I want you to notice what happened here today. I asked you two questions, and for one, you were able to very deeply describe to me what you needed and wanted, but in the other you could not. On the one hand, you chose life, and on the other you chose safety, and you cannot have safety and life at the same time. Life is connecting with your emotions and allowing yourself to feel the pain, so that channel is now open for you. The other is not."

So, it wasn't without a little bit of shame that I walked back into Dr. Okin's office ten years later realizing that in choosing Daniel, I had chosen safety, not life. And while I had had many profound breakthroughs during my original year of therapy, I was unable to resist the insidious pull into recreating the narcissistic/codependent dynamic between my parents. I felt like a bad student who had not learned her lesson—and he did not let me off the hook. A few sessions in, our time apart melted away, and in an instant the chase was on.

"So, help me understand what you were thinking when you decided to marry Daniel."

"I'm not sure I understand what you're asking." I stared blankly at him. *What was I thinking? I was thinking I wanted to get married, I suppose. Geez, take it easy,* I thought.

"You're telling me you didn't realize he had these issues before you were married?"

"Well, not really, I mean, there were signs, but I wasn't really sure . . ."

Like the expert he was, he tore down my thinly veiled excuses one by one. This was familiar territory for me with him. The more he leaned in to me, the more evasive I became, not intentionally but as a self-protecting mechanism. I numbed out. Sensing this,

Dr. Okin upped the ante and started to close in. He was not going to let me squirm out of this, and I knew it. I loved him and hated him at the same time.

"How could you have done this? You knew—you saw that he wasn't capable of giving you the life that you wanted. Now look where you are. You really fucked this up, didn't you?"

I raised my eyes to meet his attack and said the only thing I could think of. "I just knew that I could do it. I knew I could handle it."

"Oh." He stopped. "I see . . ." he said now, lowering his head, his voice softening. "You thought, 'I know what this is.' You recognized it, and you went with what you knew."

"Yes . . ." I whispered, my heart beating in my ears, realizing my year of therapy had not prevented me from repeating the cycle of codependency from my childhood. Choosing Daniel meant I could stay safely hidden emotionally, as his problems would be a great and very valid excuse for me not to have to look at my own shit.

"I'm sorry," I uttered, unable to look at his face.

"What are you sorry for?" he asked.

I should have known I couldn't say something like that without his going after me, but I was exhausted at this point. "I guess I didn't learn my lesson the first time, did I? I have needs, and I didn't choose an equal partner who could meet those needs."

"Yes." He paused before adding, "I'm sorry I couldn't get you here sooner."

I nodded. The chase was over. We had landed into this truth; no more words were necessary.

CHAPTER 7

LEARNING TO BE HUMAN

"We are not human beings trying to be spiritual.
We are spiritual beings trying to be human."
—Jacquelyn Small

I chose safety in my personal life, but I didn't choose safety at work. At work, I was fierce. Even when I was afraid, I jumped into the deep end of the pool, took risks, and spoke my mind—and I was definitely afraid at times. My heart pounded when I challenged a peer on not being transparent in his intentions on a project or stood up to Pat for something I believed in—an effort that took sustained attention. With Pat, like many CEOs I have worked with, I had to figure out how to flank and re-approach him several times from many angles to get my point across, but I was always up for the challenge. I started talking to Pat about rearticulating our company values, for example, a good two years before he allowed my team to consider revising them. It was a slow, iterative process where we continued to show him how the existing "guiding principles" that he had articulated more than eight years earlier were no longer relevant and that few people actually even knew what they were. Perhaps I used work as an outlet for all the pent-up energy I kept tamped down in my personal life; perhaps I did it because it was easier for me to do right by others than it was to do right by myself. Whatever the reason, I had such clarity when it came to what was needed for people to do great work—they need to be supported and they need to be held accountable in equal measure, and somehow I intuitively knew where that balance was. *Firm yet kind, direct yet curious* were words used to describe me throughout my tenure at Peet's. Why was I unable to achieve that balance at home? It was as if I was afraid of my power in my personal life. At work, I had no problem taking up space and seeking the truth, but at home, I would allow myself to be deceived, looking the other way when Daniel offered a lame excuse for his glassy eyes. At home, I made myself small. The revelation I had with Dr. Okin was that I actually gave away my power at home and then resented the fact that my needs were not being met despite having set up that exact dynamic.

During one of our weekly sessions, I sat feeling dejected and depressed, the full weight of what I had been doing all my life really landing on me.

"What are you thinking?" Dr. Okin asked, leaning in to try to get me to raise my head so he could look me in the eyes.

"How could I have not seen this?" I asked, looking up and shifting my gaze out the window beside me. "I am smart. I made smart choices. I assess people's strengths and weaknesses all day long. How could I have missed this?"

"You didn't miss anything," he responded. "In fact, you found exactly what you were searching for and went with what you knew, with what felt familiar to you. You recreated the relationship your mom and dad had. It's very much a subconscious process."

Of course, I thought. My diagnosis skills were not broken; on the contrary, they were like a heat-seeking missile. The problem was I was working off an old script—the one that kept me strong and capable yet emotionally isolated.

I began to read about the codependent/narcissistic attraction and saw that I had fallen right into it with my relationship with

Daniel. Reading through the list of common symptoms was like going through a history of my personal life. *Indecisiveness*, check: I had run away from two engagements before marrying Daniel. *The chronic need to "help" or "fix*," big fat check. *The impulse to "rescue*," check, check, check. One description by psychologist Dr. Ross Rosenberg that made my stomach turn was that "codependents were nice, responsible, loving people with weak and stunted boundaries." At work, these codependent qualities helped me excel, but at home, they led me straight into a disastrous state.

In the months after Daniel's death, the neat division between my home life and my professional began to crumble. It was getting harder and harder to keep up my Chinese wall, and my ability to compartmentalize was weakening by the day.

One day as I was having lunch with the head of retail operations, who had lost her husband seven years earlier, she told me that it would take a good two years to work through my loss. I stared at her blankly.

"Two years? No . . ." I said out loud, drawing out the "o." I poked at my salad, thinking to myself, *Two years for losers maybe, but not for me.*

"I know." She paused but continued, "I didn't think it would take me that long either, but it does, you'll see." She smiled as if she could read my thoughts and took a sip of her iced tea.

I was absolutely certain this woman was 100 percent wrong. I was already back at work—if not fully functioning, at least partially so. I was usually okay if I stuck to my core group of constituents who worked at my speed, but if I had to work with people outside of my normal circle, I did begin to notice that my emotional fuse had become very short. My ability to hold back my frustration had weakened. There was one woman in particular who was a director in our retail group with whom I found I couldn't spend any amount of time. Everything about her irritated me: the questions she asked, her inability to move more quickly, the way she became so perplexed at the slightest problem. Sitting with her in meetings,

I would think, *What is your problem? This is not that complicated.* Though I never said anything out loud, I'm sure she could feel the disdain I had for her. I would later come to understand that my judgment was due to her obvious display of what I viewed as weakness—something I had denied myself my entire life. She was delicate and inarticulate and overtly emotional when she was struggling with a particular topic, and I found myself silently judging her every step of the way. *Hold it together for God's sake,* I thought. *Shall I get a fainting couch for you?*

This woman's overt display of vulnerability grated on me as I pushed mine further down. I wouldn't allow myself one moment of weakness. I couldn't. I had a very real sense that if I allowed even a drop of the anguish I held inside me to come out, I wouldn't be able to push it back down again. I imagined a gushing sea of repressed and unexamined memories cresting over the floodgates and drowning me in the unbearable pain I had been hiding from for over forty years. Falling apart had never been an option for me, so my instinct was to try to intellectualize myself through my grief, carefully bypassing my heart.

Turns out, this doesn't work.

As winter made its way to spring, I came home one evening to find a white business envelope from the medical examiner's office in the pile of mail that Marci had laid on the kitchen counter. Here, at long last, was the toxicology report, the answer to what had actually happened to Daniel. I had been pressing the question down for months, ignoring it, beating it back. I waited until Nadia was in bed and I was alone before I pulled it out of the pile to look at it again. I sat on the edge of my bed and turned the letter around in my hands, not wanting to open it. I slipped my index finger under a gap in the flap and slowly ripped the top of the envelope off. I stared at the words, not able to take anything in until I anchored on "cause of death." I followed the line to the right and read, "accidental overdose." The report showed that Daniel had toxic levels of a deadly mixture of drugs and alcohol in his system. My stomach turned sour and I felt frozen in time. *Of course. Of course.* How could it be anything else? I couldn't concentrate on the details of the report, but my eyes narrowed in on that one line: *"Cause of death: accidental overdose."* I lay down on my bed, unable to move. Here it was right before my eyes, the truth I had been denying since probably the day I met Daniel. I felt nauseous and curled up into a ball, dropping the letter in the process. I fell asleep with my clothes on.

When I awoke the next morning, I picked the letter off the ground and decided to call the toxicologist after getting Nadia off to school so I could better understand what some of the terms were in the report. There was a long list of chemical names that I didn't understand, and I so badly wanted to understand. He told me from the looks of it that Daniel most likely had a heart attack and fell onto the floor, unable to get up on his own.

"Was it the head wound that killed him?" I asked. "It looked like he hit his head against the bathtub when he fell. Do you think if someone was there and had called an ambulance, it would have made a difference?" Really, what I was asking was, *Could I have saved him if I were there?* I wanted to believe that my high functioning get-it-done competence could have extended to saving my husband.

"It's hard to say," the examiner said, "but I don't think so."

My absolute certainty that my iron will could deal with anything life could throw at me suddenly seemed to fall away.

My mind wandered back to December 4. I thought about being at work while Daniel lay dying. What must he have been thinking in the moments before his death, lying supine on the bathroom floor, his head bleeding? Did he know he was dying? Was he scared? How long did it take? *Wait. Wait. Oh my God,* I thought. *I know exactly the moment it happened. I felt exactly the moment it happened.*

In the days after I learned of Daniel's death, I tried to reconstruct his movements, trying to piece together the exact moment of his death. I had last spoken with him on Monday night, December 3, and he was supposed to pick Nadia up from school on Tuesday,

December 4, but he didn't. I was able to find out from a friend who worked at Yahoo that he had logged on to his e-mail at 9:30 a.m. on December 4. I picked up his cell phone and figured out how to check his voicemail, noting that unanswered voice messages started around 12:30 p.m. Based on these two data points, I assumed he must have died Tuesday morning sometime between 9:30 a.m. and 12:30 p.m. Thinking back on that day, I remembered that I was meeting with Pat to review my board presentation scheduled the next day. As he was giving me feedback on the presentation, I remember the overwhelming rush of sadness that took me over. I began to cry. In the meeting. I began to cry in a meeting with my boss. I remember being so confused. *What's happening? This isn't me. I don't cry in meetings. I hardly even cry.* At first, I wasn't sure what was happening. I couldn't control it, so I tried to push it down—my default coping mechanism automatically kicking in. But the pain in my heart was so severe that the harder I tried, the more the pressure pushed up, up, up until I couldn't contain it anymore and I burst into sobs. Pat stopped in his tracks.

"What's the matter?" he asked, stunned. "Hey, just forget my comments, it's fine, you'll be fine . . ." He was at a loss, thinking I was crying because of the feedback he was giving me.

"Um, okay, I'm sorry . . ." was all I could muster. Shuffling my papers, I walked out of his office confused and crushed by the weight of this sadness.

As I hung up the phone with the medical examiner, I realized that must have been the exact moment that Daniel died. *My heart knew. My body knew.* I felt the sadness even though I could not make sense of that reality with my mind.

There were many similar instances of impossible-to-explain, heart-based connections that happened that year. For months after Daniel's death, for example, the lights in my living room would mysteriously dim and then get bright all by themselves. They had not done this before Daniel's death, and it always seemed to happen when we were speaking about him.

Nadia began to regularly say out loud, "Daddy, we're sorry we couldn't catch you." The lights would flicker behind her as she sobbed, and I would just hold her, feeling utterly helpless as to what to do. She also began whimpering at night in her sleep, calling out, "Daddy, Daddy!" I would go to her and hold her, trying to calm her, but it was really hard for me to emotionally stay with her in the midst of her open emotional grieving. I would force myself to stay with her physically, but inside, emotionally, I wanted to jump out of my skin; I just wanted to run away from the pain the way I had my whole life.

But my love for Nadia was greater than my resistance to the pain. For the first time in my life, love overcame fear. I could not—would not—leave my daughter in her moment of need, even if I was emotionally ill-equipped. I did my best to comfort her, mouthing the words I knew intellectually I was supposed to say while desperately trying to keep the wall up to protect my heart. I tried to separate my grieving from hers. As a mother, I needed Nadia to process her pain, knowing it was the only way for her to get through her grief, but I didn't know how to do it for myself. Sitting with her, rocking back and forth, I felt the dissonance inside me grow, threatening to split me in two. I marveled at her ability to feel and let out her emotions raw and uncensored, and at the same time, I felt deep shame in my inability to even stay with my feelings, let alone release them. I was simultaneously in awe of her and feeling deeply inadequate to the task at hand.

One day as I was wishing inside that I could take all these bad feelings and put them in a box, an idea popped into my head—something I hoped could help both me and Nadia. I devised a way for Nadia to get her feelings out that also gave me something to do with all my sadness—the Daddy Box. I took a well-made storage box that was covered with beautiful green felt and told Nadia this is where we would put the things that remind us of Daddy. I explained that we could also write him letters and put them in the box, and when we felt sad, we could look through the box to remind us of all the things we loved about Daddy. She liked this idea and immediately started to gather items from her room to put into the Daddy Box—a carved piece of wood that said "Dan" that Daniel had made in woodshop in high school; the "daddy angel," a six-inch-tall ceramic figurine of a young boy on his knees praying; framed pictures of the two of them. She grabbed her "daddy blanket," a white blanket with the bedtime prayer "Now I lay me down to sleep" in blue needlepoint script that Daniel's mother had made for him with when he was a baby, but I told her she should probably keep that one out.

An evening ritual began to develop for us. We would finish dinner and after Nadia got ready for bed, she would run and get the Daddy Box. I would ask her what she wanted to tell Daddy, and I would write it down verbatim on Post-it Notes and then put them safely in the box.

"What should I say, Mommy?" she would ask.

"Do you want to tell him how much you love him?" I would suggest.

"Yes, say that and then say, 'We wish you dear to life.'"

She would often have so many phrases I did not understand, but I dutifully wrote everything down, and when we were finished, she would pick up the daddy angel and kiss it to say good night.

As part of our evening ritual, we also read the "daddy books," three picture books I had made for the three Father's Days that Daniel had been a father on this earth. Nadia would ask me to go through them with her and to share stories about the pictures in the books. It's as if she knew she would forget and was trying hard to create memories through my stories. One night as we went through the third and most recent book I had given him less than one year earlier, I noticed on the last page there was a picture of Nadia hugging him really tight around the neck and a message I had written: "Remember, Daddy, the days are long, but the years are short." I remembered how he had cried when we gave him this book only weeks before he told us he was leaving. I remember being touched at how moved he was but now realized those tears were because he knew he would soon be leaving. How blind I had been. I didn't see a hint of the tragedy coming our way.

The Daddy Box rituals I devised to help Nadia work through her feelings began to help me too. Slowly, slowly, with Nadia showing me the way, I began to feel. At first, it was a simple tinge of sadness that I would quickly brush away, but I knew I had felt it. Over time, as I saw that feeling my pain wasn't going to kill me, I began to allow myself a few moments of sorrow. I would cry by myself and in front of Nadia because I knew she wouldn't judge me. What I didn't see at the time was that I was my own harshest critic. The only person judging me was in fact me.

At work, the more I began to feel, the more other people began to notice. One day at work, one of the directors on my team gave me a smile and a look that said, "I feel for you." I had a fine working relationship with this man, but he was not someone I felt I could really open up with. I smiled back at him, remembering how just a few months earlier in November when word got out that Daniel had moved out, I had mentioned to him that I thought Daniel might be using. A recovered addict himself, he told me that he would be happy to sit down and speak with me. But of course, that conversation never happened, and here we were a mere few months later looking at each other awkwardly.

"We never did have that conversation, did we?" he asked gently.

"No, I guess we didn't. I never thought it could get so bad so quickly," I said, my feeble response trailing off into thin air.

"Do you know how it happened?"

I nodded. "I just got the toxicology report." I paused, my heart pounding. I felt the resistance but managed to push myself to go deeper. "Accidental overdose. He had pills, alcohol, and cocaine in his system. I think it started when he had a bike accident on our first anniversary, and he started taking pain pills; I think he never stopped." This was the first time I admitted this out loud. I held my breath, waiting for judgment, but to my surprise, what I got was understanding.

"You know," he said, "there are certain combinations of drugs that people end up becoming addicted to that can quickly devolve into a dangerous downward spiral. One is meth and pot, which was what I did, and the other is cocaine and alcohol. One is a stimulant and the other a depressant, so while it may not be intuitive, using the two together allows you to keep using around the clock."

After our conversation, I began to read more about this lethal mix and learned that combining cocaine use with alcohol can cause death from overdose at cocaine levels that are only one tenth of those known to be fatal with cocaine alone. Later studies reported that the risk of sudden death—*sudden death*—is twenty times greater for use of cocaine and alcohol together than it is for cocaine alone. I sat with this fact for a long time. I realized that it must explain how Daniel's death happened so quickly. I wondered if he knew he was putting himself in such acute danger. I teetered between fact and feeling in many other ways, but in this one, I stayed firmly on the factual side. It was all too much to bear.

In all other ways, I was on an emotional roller coaster as I tried to make sense of everything that had happened. For a long time, I was angry at Daniel's family for not giving him the love and the wherewithal to make better decisions in his life. Then I was mad at Daniel because after all, ultimately you are responsible for your own actions. Then I was mad at myself because deep in my heart I knew he was in trouble, but I didn't reach out to help. My anger and grief came in waves—big waves that crushed me and spun me around, letting me go just when I thought I had run out of air, only to pull me down again. Other times, they came as gentle, ripple tides that delicately washed over my feet in the sand. Round and round I went—huge waves crashing upon me, pulling me under until I thought I would drown, and when the anger receded, the sadness returned. At home, Nadia and I took solace in each other. No sooner had she moved into her big-girl bed than she moved back into my bed and stayed there for two years.

I was exhausted by the end of each workday and usually ended up staying in bed with Nadia after holding her to go to sleep. One night after I was certain she was asleep, I turned on my overhead light and gazed over to the stack of books on my bedside table that I had been purchasing on near-death experiences and life after death in my ongoing attempt to "understand death." My bookshelf looked like the self-help section of the local bookstore. I picked up a book called *The Sacred Purpose of Being Human* by Jacquelyn Small, where she asserts that we are not human beings trying to be spiritual but rather spiritual beings trying to be human. The idea that I was an ethereal, spiritual being struggling with how to be a human on this earth rather than an intellectual, earth-bound human trying to achieve enlightenment touched me deeply, but I didn't realize why until I started reading. She used the word "psychospiritual" to refer to the process of transformation. "These are the tools and processes that access the whole self, not just the intellect and not just your emotions." I gasped audibly when I read this, knowing in my bones this was true, but what did it mean exactly? I read on. "Each of our seven chakras represents a distinct level of consciousness. The first three chakras are all about the ego and fall in the realm of traditional psychology. It's what roots us as humans. The fourth chakra is your heart," she says, "and the process of transformation starts by opening our hearts by creating a bridge to higher consciousness." *What is this? Is this what I'm doing?* I felt like I had been lost in the forest and had stumbled upon a map with a big gold star that said, "You are here."

She went on to say that reconnecting with our authentic self requires accessing the last three chakras, and the only way we do this is through an open heart. "You must be centered in your Self to access your higher power; an unbalanced ego can't get there." So, the work I was doing with Dr. Okin was really focused on the first three chakras and were now getting me to a place where I could open my heart. I knew in that moment that I was being called to continue the journey. Immediately after having this thought, I read, "The realization that your nature is both human and divine leads you to see that the transformer of your consciousness is always within you." Shivers ran up my spine and I felt light-headed. "Thank you," I said out loud. "Thank you." This was the clarity I needed to commit to going deeper even if I still didn't fully understand what a chakra was.

Suddenly, everything I was reading made sense, and little by little I started to understand that despite my outward display of strength, inside I was a big fat scaredy-cat; finally, I had enough courage to admit this to myself. By the end of the summer it was getting harder and harder to try to feel my way through my grief, balance my weekly sessions with Dr. Okin with being a newly single parent, and have a big job. I was much more aware that I was straddling two worlds and I didn't want to do it anymore. My mind was swirling with all the ideas in the books I had been reading, and I needed time and space to process them. My energy at work continued to decline, and to make matters worse, 2008 was proving to be the most difficult economic environment since the Great Depression. It seemed like all of a sudden, everything got really hard.

I walked into Pat's office toward the end of summer and said, "I think I need to take a break. I'm finding it harder and harder to stay engaged, and I think I need to unplug and allow myself time to decompress a little." I assured him that my team could pick up the slack and could do without me for a month or so. The truth was I had been leaning on them more and more since my return, so I knew they were more than capable.

Without hesitation, Pat told me to go ahead and take the time. I almost think he might have been waiting for me to get to this point.

The first week of my six weeks off was spent on organizing my life—running all the errands I never had time for and doing the pet projects around the house I never had time to do, including burning all my CDs on to my computer. We were officially into the digital age. I was like a tornado going through the house, and it wasn't until Marci commented about my frenetic state that I realized I wasn't doing what I said I wanted to be doing during my time off, which was to slow down and be more introspective. "Being" was so much harder than "doing" for me. Another friend made an idle comment one day that we are human beings, not human doings. *We are human beings*, I thought, *but how do you just "be"?* I decided to try yoga and started reading a new book called *The Untethered Soul* by Michael Singer. The combination of those two things over the following month succeeded in slowing me down.

The *Untethered Soul* begins by talking about how our mind and all the thoughts we generate, including the criticisms—the *shoulds* and *coulds*—are all man-made and that this is what causes our suffering. *Hmm, maybe this book isn't for me*, I thought. I had always been able to rise above the noise in my head, so this message wasn't really resonating with me. Then I went on to read that the way we stay away from our suffering is by distracting ourselves with the outer world. *Hold on a minute.* That sounded a little more familiar. Michael Singer asserts that we use the outer world to distract us from what's happening inside; that is, we try to control our external environment to stay away from the thoughts and feelings inside that are painful. *This* I could understand. My body was buzzing as I read this, so I knew it was true. Not only had I been distracting myself my whole life, but most of the time, I didn't even know I was doing it. *Was my ability to rise above my inner voice my gift or my curse?*

If *Sacred Purpose* introduced the idea that spiritual transformation was only possible through the heart, *The Untethered Soul* taught me exactly how to do it. Singer writes that it is only in leaning into the resistance that we will find true happiness. He claims it is your resistance that is the source of suffering, not the pain itself. This was so counterintuitive for me, but I stayed with this idea and tried to notice when I resisted ideas or thoughts in my life, and then I tried to stay with the fear and the discomfort that arose from staying with that resistance. "Lean into the resistance" became my mantra—and I was willing to do it because I now understood I was on a spiritual journey.

———————

When I returned to work six weeks later in October, the U.S. economy was in a full-blown recession. The real estate bubble had burst, banks were hoarding cash, so the credit markets were frozen, and the Fed was in the midst of loaning billions of dollars to bail out banks and financial institutions as they tried to prevent a complete economic collapse. Most everyone I knew had lost 40 to 50 percent of their savings, and for the first time ever, we began to discuss a possible layoff at Peet's.

It only took a few days back at the office to realize that my team had not only stepped up, but they had completely filled any of the role I had been playing in operationalizing our HR strategy. As I tried to reintegrate back into my role, it felt as if I kept bumping into my team members. "Oh, you've got that? Okay. No need to follow up on this decision? All right. Oh, you absorbed that into your process? I see." It was a little unsettling at first. Had I worked myself out of a job? But as the effects of the difficult economic environment on our business began to play out, and I started spending more and more time with my counterparts across the organization, I realized my team had handed me a gift: the opportunity to step up and be a true senior leader. After a year of being in the weeds, hiring my lieutenants, restructuring the team, and building out the HR capability, I had a fully functioning department, and they didn't need me to be in the details anymore. What they needed was someone to step up and play point with the executive leadership team.

Personality-wise, it worked very well as I had a team of introverts who really didn't like dealing with challenging executives. I, on the other hand, was an extrovert, a well-rested fighter, and for the first time in my life I had developed the ability to be a little more present and grounded in my heart. We began to work together in a beautifully complementary way where I was able to let go of the details and trust in my team to meet our deliverables while I shifted my focus outward and cross-functionally, removing obstacles, greasing the skids, and providing air cover when necessary. In turn, they focused on producing amazing work that ultimately reflected positively on me too.

The conversations I was having with people started to take on greater depth. I was more patient after my six weeks off. I had more emotional wherewithal to stay with difficult conversations. I paid attention to the context of the conversations as much as the content. I noticed when someone agreed with a direction but looked agitated and unconvinced. Rather than driving toward a particular outcome in the way I had always done, I noticed that I could make more space to allow things to unfold more organically. I was more curious. I asked questions. All of a sudden, I was saying things like, "Is there anything else you think is important for us to know before we move forward on this?" when I sensed hesitation. Baby steps. It would take some time for me to find the balance between what I perceived as pushing or "willing" things to happen and allowing them to unfold naturally. What I didn't realize at the time is there is a beautiful middle ground where you are neither striving and swimming upstream or abdicating all responsibility and becoming a victim—a place and space where you dance with life as a co-creator to what unfolds. This required that I continue to listen to the signals coming from my heart and from my body and to quiet my mind, so that the noise of my always-on brain didn't drown out important messages.

As a leader, I started to notice that moving away from being a "helper" and "fixer" required a shift away from my traditional hero persona, which had kept me emotionally distant and above it all. This was the real gift my team gave me. They didn't need me to help or fix anything because they were fully capable of doing their jobs themselves. Letting go of my hero persona was what finally allowed me to bring some softness and vulnerability into my work—to start showing up more authentically.

On December 4, 2008, the one-year anniversary of Daniel's death, I could barely get out of bed. I felt heavy, dull, my head hurt, and it wasn't until mid-morning that I realized what day it was. I went to work like a good little soldier, but I could barely make it through lunch. When I called my friend, Anh, she told me she had arranged a massage for me at the Claremont Hotel that afternoon. I exhaled deeply as I collapsed on the massage table mid-afternoon, grateful not to have to concentrate on life anymore. Strange how my heart and body sensed the very day of Daniel's loss before my mind did. I was beginning to wake up to a new way of seeing things—noticing things about myself, like how scared I was underneath all my outer strength. *Maybe Daniel's death was my wake-up call, to get real, to bring down my defenses, to listen to that voice inside and allow myself to feel.* It was getting harder and harder for me to compartmentalize my feelings—harder still to push them down and pretend I didn't have any. I was in unchartered waters but knew that I had drifted too far from shore to go back to how I used to be. Ever so slowly, I began to peel back the layers, one by one by one, trying to find my way to the real me. It helped that the nation was in economic mourning with the recession, so the mood of the nation reflected my own, which no doubt helped my burgeoning introspection. I was learning how to lean into the resistance, but it would take another life tragedy to push me to an even deeper awakening.

Chapter 8

REMOVING THE ARMOR

*"Courage is not the absence of fear
but the ability to walk through it."*
—Mark Twain

Communication with my mom and dad had become more and more infrequent after Daniel's death. It was uncomfortable for all of us, and I didn't have the energy to pretend that everything was fine in the way that I had always done before his passing. In May of 2009, a few months after the one-year anniversary of Daniel's death, I called my mom, realizing I hadn't spoken with her in over a month. During our call, in a very offhand tone of voice, she happened to say, "Your father is in the hospital."

I paused, trying to make sense of what I had heard. "Sorry, what? What's he in the hospital for?"

"He's been having problems breathing."

I pictured an outpatient clinic, an appointment. "So, he's there for some tests, you mean?"

"No, he's actually in the hospital," she said. There was an awkward pause, and I realized she was not offering any more information.

"Mom, what's going on?" I asked. Despite the increase in my blood pressure, I resisted raising my voice in anger because I knew my mother would shut down, but inside I was screaming at her. *WTF, Mom, are you kidding me? Why didn't you call to tell me? Were you even going to let me know?* Instead, I pushed down my anger and calmly asked, "How long has he been in the hospital, and how long do you expect him to stay there?" I was trying to keep my voice steady, betraying the sirens that were going off in my head.

"I'm not sure . . ." she said, her voice trailing off.

I wanted to scream but maintained control and squeezed out a terse, "Okay, I'll make plans to come to Vegas."

"Yes," she said, "that would be good, I think."

When I shared with my team at work that my father was in the hospital, I could see the concern in their eyes, but no one said a word. What was there to say? We were here not so long ago with Daniel. I booked a flight to Las Vegas that weekend, taking Friday off and leaving Nadia at home with Marci. When I arrived, I called my mother and learned she was at home, so I decided to go straight to the hospital to see my father. I wanted to be alone with him. When I found his room, my knees buckled. He looked so frail. He was completely hooked up to machines and intubated, so he could not speak. As I gingerly approached his bedside, I couldn't shake the feeling that he would open his eyes any moment and give me that wry grin as if to say, *I'm tricking them all; I'm not really sick!* Was this my version of magical thinking? My inability or unwillingness to see him in such a fragile state? Or was it more my inability to trust him? Ever since I had overheard him speak coherently to his friend after Daniel's death, I didn't trust that his mental acuity was as low as it appeared. It seemed like he was faking it on some level, like he understood much more than he let on. In that moment, I realized that he had been much sicker than I had admitted to myself and even considered that his lack of awareness might have been due more to his self-medicating than his declining health.

I held my father's hand. It was so soft yet stiff.

"Dad, it's Laila. I'm here." I looked for any sign of acknowledgment, but I didn't think he heard me. I stayed with him a long time, patting his hand, trying to make sense of the fact that my dad was lying intubated and unconscious in a hospital bed and trying to untangle the knot of complicated feelings rushing through me.

I suspect every girl thinks her father is handsome, but mine really, truly was. He was this exotic mix of James Dean and Jack Lord from the old seventies' TV series *Hawaii Five-0*, a little like a young Elvis back in the fifties. He had dark hair he slicked back with pomade his entire life, gray eyes, and fine, straight features. He always had a look on his face like he had a secret, the corner of his mouth turned up in a half smile, a gleam in his eye. I know that he was empirically good-looking because women talked about it freely, from my cousins to my friends to women passing us on the street. But as charming as he was outside our home, inside he was a hard man, a force of nature as unpredictable as the weather. My early childhood memories of him were twofold: either he was quiet and distant, in which case we all walked on eggshells so as not to trigger his rage, or he was exploding molten hot lava and you took cover so as not to be a casualty. The primary object of his anger and disdain was usually my mother. She couldn't do anything right. Even when they weren't fighting you could feel the contempt they had toward one another. This set up a cold war between them and left me to choose sides.

I had always yearned for my father to be proud of me, to see me, to love me, yet I had very few memories of us connecting in any meaningful way. Most of my childhood memories were centered on the really big fights my parents had. One particular fight etched in my memory is when I was six and my father was trying to teach my little brother a lesson—he was just two years old at the time. Apparently, my brother had left a piece of pita bread on the floor, and my father wanted him to put it in the ashtray.

"Pick up the pita bread and put it into the ashtray," he demanded, only inches from my brother's tiny face.

My brother put his hand in his mouth, began to suck on it, and looked up at my mother with tears in his eyes. But my father told my mother to stay out of it, so she refused to help my brother but instead began yelling at my father to stop being so hard on him. Over and over my father took the piece of pita bread out of the ashtray and commanded my brother to put it in himself, and the angrier he became, the more scared my brother became, until he was crying uncontrollably. Hiding behind a nearby sofa, I had been silently pleading for my brother to pick up the piece of bread so that the screaming and the crying could end. I finally ran out, picked up the piece of pita bread, threw it into the ashtray, and dove back behind the sofa. My father looked up at me, clearly annoyed, flicked the piece of pita bread back out of the ashtray, and resumed his assault on my brother.

As mean as my father could be, I wanted to be like him—strong and powerful. But aligning too closely with my father meant losing my mother, so I learned to be in both camps: aligned enough with my father that I received preferential treatment for my strength and bravery, but also there for my mother as her confidante and, as I grew, ultimately her protector. This balancing act was tested in small ways punctuated by big fights that were burned into my core memories forever. One such incident was when I was nine or ten years old and my parents were fighting late one night after I had gone to bed. I was silently praying in my bed, bargaining with God that I would be a better person—I would clean my room, I would help my mother more—if He would just please make them stop fighting. I clamped my hands together in prayer and was sure that if I could keep them that way, my prayer would have more power behind it.

Suddenly, I heard glass break, a crash, and my mother screaming my name: "Laila, I need you!"

I shot out of bed and ran to her. She was lying on the floor in the dining room just behind the table. My father had thrown a gold-rimmed drinking glass at her and it crashed through the window behind her. My father was standing in the living room, breathing heavily with a wild look in his eyes, when he saw me enter the room and go straight for my mother. I kneeled on the lime-green shag carpet and helped my mother up. She leaned against me, disoriented and scared, and I saw that her scalp had been cut. The crown of her head was oozing blood, and I tried to remove the matted hair and gold shards that were sticking to the cut. I could feel my mother relax into my arms, and as she closed her eyes, she squeezed out silent tears.

"It's okay, Mommy, I'm here," I said. "It's okay, you're going to be okay."

I looked up at my father with as much resolve as I could muster in that moment. *It's over,* I said with my eyes. As I got my mother up into a chair to better tend to her wound, my father retreated into the bedroom.

The next day, I went with my mother to the doctor's office. I heard her trying to explain away what had happened, making excuses for my father. I was so embarrassed for her. The doctor looked at me to see if I had anything to add, but I felt my mother's icy stare, so I averted the doctor's gaze. When I looked up again, I saw him shake his head with a resigned air of judgment as he finished dressing her wound. He glanced at me again with a mixture of sadness and pity, and I felt red-hot shame as the evidence of our broken family life was on display for the doctor to see.

Over time, I began to begrudge my mother because she was weak and unable to protect us from my father's outbursts. But instead of taking issue with my father for his violent and unpredictable behavior, I was resentful of my mother for her passivity. Eventually, I stepped into that role myself. I became the fighter, the protector, the strong one, and my father knew it. In a strange way, it bonded us to each other because he respected the fact that I wouldn't allow myself to be pushed around, and I think that over time, he took less issue with me than with my brother and sister. We lived in a delicate, unspoken détente of sorts. *You stay out of my way, and I'll stay out of yours.* When he came home from work, I would retreat into my room, claiming I had homework. If he lost his temper with my mother, I would look him silently in the eye before retreating to my room. I would allow him his outbursts within reason, but he knew I would jump in if I felt real danger afoot. Once, when I was fourteen years old, I did.

That year, I was an eighth-grader, and I remember working on homework just before dinner when I heard my father raise his voice out in the family room. Fear rose up through my body, flooding my arms and legs with adrenaline as was normally the case at the beginning of each of these episodes. *Please don't let this be a bad one,* I prayed. *I'm not in the mood for this tonight.* But it was not to be. All of a sudden, the voices got louder, and I could hear clearly what my father was saying.

"I don't need you; *you* need me! If you don't like it, you can hit the door!" The only thing that somewhat alleviated the tension of that moment was the dark humor of his inadvertent mixed metaphor. *What's he trying to say?* I thought. *Hit the road? Walk out the door?* He slammed his fist onto the table and repeated this over and over. It sounded like my mother walked away from him, but as his voice got louder, I understood that he was following her, reciting these words and trying to get into her face. He repeated these words so many times—"I don't need you," he kept saying, "you need me! I don't need you; *you* need me!"—but then he changed his position and said, "If you don't like it, I can leave!"

At this, I snapped. I stormed out of my room and went into the kitchen to see for myself what was happening. My father continued his tirade, barely aware of my presence. I leaned over the kitchen counter, and in complete and abject terror, I raised my voice to my father and said, "Then why don't you just leave then? We don't need you. Just leave."

The silence in that moment was deafening. My mother, who was standing between my father and me, looked up in shock. My father looked down as he rose from his seat in the den and began to walk toward me. I could see his lips were moving, but my heart was beating so loudly in my ears I couldn't make out what he was saying. He wasn't yelling anymore, which made me more scared, and I braced myself for what he might do to me. To my shock and relief, my father turned back into his bedroom, packed a bag, and left, slamming the front door in a rage. I stood frozen, unable to speak, as the house fell silent. My brother and sister slowly came out of their rooms like ants after a rainstorm, looking around cautiously to make sure our father wasn't still in the house. I had done it! I had defeated the monster. David had defeated Goliath! When the shock wore off, I felt lighter. I could breathe. I wasn't afraid anymore.

Over the next few days, after my father left, I immediately took over the leadership of the household, creating my own rules around mealtimes and dinner menus. My mother was strangely indifferent during these first few days, and I couldn't understand why she wasn't as jubilant as I was.

"Mom, what should we make for dinner tonight?" I asked her the day after my father had left. She simply smiled at me and didn't answer. I was irritated by her unresponsiveness but also a little worried. *What does she know that I don't?* I wondered. A lot, as it turns out, because a mere three days later, my father returned home. I was in my bedroom getting dressed for my basketball game, putting my things in my gym bag and pulling my hair up into a ponytail when I heard him enter the house. Panic rose inside me. *Shit, what's he doing here?* I knew this was not going to bode well for me. Soon, my mother came back into my room and told me that my father wanted to speak with me. I refused.

"No," I said, "I don't want to talk to him." I continued to brush out my ponytail, refusing to follow her.

"Laila, it's not really a request. You need to go out there and say you're sorry."

"What? Me? Say sorry? For what? I didn't do anything! He's the one that was yelling and screaming, saying he wanted to leave. I just told him that he could."

"Yes, but he's your father, and you need to respect him. Just go out and say you're sorry, or I'm afraid he will not let you go to your game."

My mind raced with options for other choices, but none came. I really didn't want to miss my game, so I put on my game face and went out to see my father. He was sitting in his usual spot on the sofa and he looked sad, not mad. I didn't quite know what to think of this. *Is this a trick?* I did not trust him. I slowly walked over to the sofa, and he pulled me down by the wrist to sit down next to him. I couldn't even look at him, so I looked down and started playing with my nails. I disconnected emotionally from him and went to a place far away. He reached over and kissed me, tears in his eyes, but I had nothing to give him. My body only stiffened and refused to reciprocate.

Mechanically and with no emotion whatsoever, I said, "I'm sorry."

He released me when it was clear I wasn't going to hug him back, and I got up and walked out of the room without looking back at him.

The tide turned for us on that day. For the first time, I showed him I could be as tough, if not tougher, than he was. I had learned at the feet of the master and had outplayed him at his game. I was sad, but I was also exhausted from contorting myself for so long to win his attention and approval. I wanted more than the crumbs of attention and affection I was able to salvage from our rare interactions. I wanted so badly not to care about him, to snub him in the way I felt he had always dismissed me. I donned the armor. It was heavy, but I was ready. In a way, I had been preparing myself for this my whole childhood. We entered another cold period in our relationship. We kept our distance from each other, each expecting the other to make the first move, but neither of us ever did. Soon enough I left home for college and never returned home outside of brief visits for the holidays.

As I stood by my father's hospital bed, the highlight reel of my childhood memories came to an end. I brushed away tears, realizing that my core memories of my father were just one big fight after another.

Was it any wonder where I got my fighting instincts? But I also realized what I had done after my father came back: at fourteen years old, I began to shut down emotionally, taking on the helper role in the house—the one who fixes things, the one who takes action, the one who does not feel. I realized I was still playing those same roles. My mother abdicated all responsibility for my father's care, and before I left Las Vegas that Sunday night, I became the primary contact with the plethora of doctors and specialists overseeing my father's treatment. As I signed my name on the forms that transferred responsibility from my mother to me, an indescribable heaviness filled my heart. I knew that I was more than capable of making these decisions, but somewhere deep inside me I still felt like that little girl being asked to take on more than she was prepared for. I flipped through the documents, signing my name and dating at the bottom until I got to a form that said "DNR" in big letters.

"Sorry, what's DNR?" I asked the ICU nurse who was sitting behind the counter waiting for me to finish signing everything.

"Oh, that stands for 'do not resuscitate.'" She paused, and when it was clear I still didn't understand, she offered, "If you choose DNR, that means the next time he goes into cardiac arrest, we won't try to keep him alive with machines."

"Has this happened already or is this standard?" I asked. What I really wanted to say was, *Are you asking me to tell you it's okay to let my dad die?*

She looked down at her notes, raised her head, and nodded, "Yes, it's happened twice since he's been with us."

My eyes welled with tears. "Um, I'm going to have to get back to you on this one." I drove back to my mother's house and asked to see my dad's will to see if he gave any indication as to what he might want. Searching through a big binder, I came upon a form that stated that my father did not wish to be kept alive by machines. I looked at the DNR form one last time and signed my name.

Two weeks after returning from visiting my father, I was sitting at a small table at a French-style bistro in Pacific Heights, interviewing a very articulate, tall blonde woman for a possible in-house general counsel position, when my cell phone rang with a Nevada 702 area code number I did not recognize. An alarm went off inside me. I smiled and held up a finger, indicating to the candidate that this would take just a minute.

"Hello," a woman said, "this is St. Rose Hospital, and we have your father, George Tarraf, here. He's asking for his family."

"I'm sorry, I don't understand. Is something wrong?" I asked.

"Well, ma'am, when our patients sense there isn't much time, they ask to see their loved ones."

My heart pounded in my chest, and I felt a rush of blood go through my body and a surge of heat go up my neck. So, he really was dying; it wasn't a trick after all. I got up from the table and walked away to speak more privately. All I could think to say was, "When?"

"I would encourage you to come as soon as you can."

I went numb. Just like that, time had run out.

I absentmindedly took my seat back at the bistro table, my heart, head, and body completely out of sync—my body feeling nauseous in reaction to the news I had just received, my heart trying to numb out so as not to feel the pain, and my head fixating on an odd daydream I used to have in which my dad and I were driving a convertible around curvy rounds hugging a mountainside and I was desperately trying to get him to hear what I was saying.

My face must have shown the level of inner dissonance I felt because the moment I sat down, my interviewee looked at me and said, "Is everything okay?" The look on her face was one of alarm, and it helped to shake me out of my reverie.

"Yes, um, my father is in the hospital, and I guess, um, he's not doing well . . ."

"Listen, you should go," she said. "My experience with these things is you need to do what's necessary right away."

She had a sense of urgency that felt like a cattle prod shocking me out of my half-dream state. I felt kicked out of the cave I was trying to hide in, not wanting to look at what was right in front of me. I drove home in a state of denial. *Not today, it's Nadia's birthday. I can't leave her on her birthday. She's only five years old.* When I got home, I saw Nadia playing with her figures on the Persian rug in the middle of the living room, many of them strewn in a halo around her. When she heard me come in she jumped over the circle of toys and threw her arms around my neck in a tight hug.

"Mommy!" she cried.

"Hi, Bug! Happy birthday, beautiful girl!"

"I'm five today!" She held up five tiny fingers, her eyes big and bright. "What are we going to do tonight for my *actual* birthday?" she asked.

We had a princess birthday party planned that weekend for Nadia. We had booked an actress who was going to come to our house dressed as Aurora from Sleeping Beauty to entertain a dozen kindergarten girls. Daniel's mother had even made the very same pink princess dress as the one Aurora would be wearing so that she and Nadia could be twins. I felt stuck. Despite the elaborate party planned in just a few days, I couldn't imagine leaving Nadia in that moment. So I called my mother and told her that she needed to go see my father. I also called my brother, who lived in Las Vegas, and suggested he go see my dad as well.

What I didn't say was that I was scared, that I was pretending that this wasn't happening. I negotiated with myself—*I will go first thing tomorrow*—but the anxiety in my body continued to escalate. After dinner, I decided to phone the hospital and asked to speak with my father. The nurse put the phone up to his ear.

"Dad? Can you hear me?" I paused but didn't hear anything from him. "Dad," I continued, "it's me. I just wanted to let you know that I'm coming tomorrow morning, okay? And Dad? I wanted to say thank you for everything. You're a good dad, and I love you very much. Okay, Dad? You need to know that, that I love you very much and I thank you for everything you've done for me in my life." I didn't know what else to say. In that moment, I could not hold on to any resentment and found myself forgiving him for all his imperfections. All I felt was love and gratitude. "Dad," I said, "Nadia would like to sing you a song, okay?" I handed Nadia the phone, and she eagerly took it from my hands.

"Hi, Papa, I'm going to sing you a song now." She launched into a French song she was learning in school and danced throughout the living room and kitchen as she sang for her grandfather. "Did you like it, Papa?" she asked as she finished. "It was in French," she added, "so maybe you didn't understand the words, but the music is nice, isn't it?" I marveled at how easily she carried herself. She looked at me as if to say, *Now what?*

I mouthed to her: "Tell him you love him." Her face lit up.

"Yes, Lion, I love you so much!"

I wiped away my tears and tried to compose myself as I took the phone back from her. Nadia and I had begun calling my father "The Lion" because he looked gruff and menacing on the outside but, like Aslan in Narnia, was strong and good on the inside.

"Goodbye, Dad," I could barely choke out. "We love you so much. I'll see you tomorrow."

I hung up the phone and booked my flight for the next day.

Very early the next morning around five o'clock, I woke up with a start. My heart raced; I felt sick. I wondered if I was getting the flu, but before I could even get out of bed, my cell phone rang next to my bed. *No. No, please no.* It was my mother.

"Laila, the hospital called. Your father just died." Her voice was soft and sad. My knees buckled as I tried to get out of bed, and I silently began to cry.

"Laila, are you there?"

"Yes, I'm here. Oh, Mom, I'm so sorry," was all I could say. I was certain that I had awoken at the moment of his death. It was bizarre how that kept on happening to me. Tuning back into the call with my mother, I asked, "Mom, were you able to go see him last night?"

"No," she said.

I was speechless. How could she not go? She was a mere two miles from the hospital.

"Do you know if Jason went to go see him?" I asked.

"I don't know," she said. I later learned that my brother did not go see my father either.

A few hours later, I kissed my little princess goodbye, grateful once again to have Marci in my life, and headed for the airport to board a plane for Las Vegas. Since Nadia was only five years old and had just started seeing a wonderful therapist to help her integrate the loss of her father, I was advised that she not attend my father's funeral. I happily obliged. I knew all too well what was coming, and she didn't need to relive this again. Looking out over the San Francisco Bay, I settled into my seat and began to feel very guilty that I had not taken a flight out just twelve hours earlier. Why hadn't I? And how could my mother not have driven the two miles between her home and the hospital to be at his bedside? The realization of just how little emotional capacity my family had hit me in the face, and how we all inherited the family trait of avoidance. All of us.

A plethora of emotions came up for me. First, shame: How could we have allowed our father to die all alone? No one deserves that. Two, anger: How could they have not gone to him? How could *I* have not gone to him? I allowed my lifelong defense mechanism of numbing out to keep me from going to his bedside the day before. Third, regret: I could have been there for him, and I missed it. Fourth, fear: Would I continue to deny the big emotional moments in my life, opting for safety instead of life? Had I not learned my lesson yet? What would it take? And lastly, resolve: I would never let this happen again. Here was my second reminder in less than two years of how precious and fleeting life is. If Daniel's death cracked the hard shell that protected my heart, my father's death dealt the fatal blow that shattered the remaining pieces and left it completely exposed. *No more hiding*, I vowed.

I leaned back in my seat and tried to get my mind around the fact that my father was no more. No more George Tarraf.

CHAPTER 9

FACING THE PAIN

*"If you bring forth what is within you, what you bring
forth will save you. If you do not bring forth what is within you,
what you do not bring forth will destroy you."*
—THOMAS MERTON

As the airplane circled in preparation for landing, I grappled with the reality of my father's death; I couldn't shake the feeling that I was on a business trip, not a deeply personal one, and for the first time in my life I began to question why this held true for me. The answer came pretty easily: *Because you're the fix-it girl, dummy.* I let out a little laugh and gazed out the window at the clouds below me. I honestly didn't mind being the person who had to deal with all of life's major moments for my family, I just didn't appreciate how it automatically defaulted to me like it was my job. At Tarraf Inc. I was the person tasked with getting things done. We all had our roles, and we had all been playing them dutifully and without question our entire lives. But now I was waking up to the dysfunction that had held us in these static roles, and I wanted to shift things around. I wanted to say, "Hey, I don't mind pulling the long oar on the administration of death—again—but could we just try to come together and talk about it? Feel a little of what's happening instead of numbing out in each of our own private, no-feel zones?" But I was so early in my process, I simply could not fathom how to begin to untie a lifetime of deeply rooted, habitual family patterns. I had my hands full working through my own little knot. *At least I get a fresh start with Nadia,* I thought. *I can make things right with her from the very beginning.*

I felt a longing in that moment to be with her—to have the easiness that we shared through our unspoken language and to feel the love that ran freely between us. I had left her at home because I was advised by her new therapist, Dr. Michael Litter, that she not be exposed to another death so soon after her father's. We had been working with Dr. Litter for close to a year, and during this time he had become a godsend to our family. Nadia met with him every week, and I would meet with Michael every two months to learn of her progress, to give him feedback on how she was doing at school and at home, and to get guidance from him on how to best handle whatever was coming up for us.

When I first took Nadia to see Dr. Litter, I couldn't help but feel a little jealous. I looked around his office filled with figurines, dolls, books, and other toys on shelves and in baskets, and asked him if he used all these things in working with Nadia.

"Yes," he said, "for kids who have suffered a big loss, before they are able to really put complex thoughts together, we use play therapy as a tool to help them express their thoughts and feelings via imagination and play. Nadia gets to come in and work through the myriad of emotions associated with her grief—confusion, anxiety, anger, and even guilt—by playing. The goal with this type of therapy is specifically to help children emerge resilient and resourceful with better coping skills and a healthier worldview."

"Do you comment on the play?" I asked, fascinated with the concept.

"No," Dr. Litter said, "it's important not to try to tidy up a child's feelings too quickly. For Nadia, giving her time to play gives her access to her heart, and as she watches her heart play, her head makes sense of it. I can't stress how critical it is for her to have the time and space to do this with me, or with a friend, because it is pure emotional thinking and insight building for her."

I smiled, nodding my head. Where was my Dr. Litter when I was young? *Can I have a do-over please?* I thought, and then I realized that maybe this *was* my do-over. Nadia and I could both learn to connect with our emotions—Nadia through Michael and me through Nadia. Instead of learning this from my mother, I would get to learn it from my daughter. The student is the master, and the master is the student.

The experience of Nadia's therapy was a constant reminder of what my default was, what was ingrained in me as a child and how I was now getting the chance to break the cycle. I remember telling Michael early in our sessions that Nadia would try to comfort me if she saw that I was sad, and he quickly advised me that I had to be very specific with her that it was not her role to comfort me.

"She's trying to step into the mother role; don't allow her to do that," he instructed.

She's a chip off the old block, I thought—and I learned that allowing her to comfort me would prevent her from fully feeling her own feelings. So, every time she tried to overstep her bounds in trying to support me, I would say, "Nadia, I'm the mommy and you're the child. Right now, it's my job to take care of you."

"But Mommy, I can help you," she would say. My heart broke to see my child ready to take on an adult's pain, and then it broke again when I realized this was exactly what I had done, only my mother didn't know enough to stop me. Consequently, I had taken on my mother's pain when I hadn't even learned how to deal with my own. No wonder I shut down emotionally; it was my survival mechanism. I vowed not to repeat that cycle.

"You will help me one day, Nadia, I promise, but first I take care of you. Don't you know that I find joy in taking care of you?" I could tell this confused her, so I explained. "I take such joy in being your mommy, which includes taking care of you and helping you to learn how to take care of yourself. Are you trying to take away my joy? Is that what you're trying to do?" I would tease her and tickle her when I said this.

"Okay, Mommy, you take care of me then." Then she would curl up in my lap and relax. Just the way it should be. I suddenly felt very proud of my little girl and of myself for the very simple fact that I was allowing her to be the child in our relationship.

With Michael's help I was able to navigate around the emotional potholes and help Nadia work through her feelings of loss. During the first year that Nadia saw Michael, she was consumed with trying to sort out what kind of world she lived in—"the good world or the bad world."

"In the bad world, everything goes wrong," Michael explained. "People die, they leave her, there's fighting, it's Armageddon, but in the good world, nobody dies, nobody gets sick, and there's a benevolent queen who rules this world."

"Am I the queen?" I asked, placing my hand on my chest.

"You most certainly are." He smiled, and I felt a surge of pride run through my body. Not only was I the adult in this relationship, but I was also seen as a powerful queen. *Yes, my daughter can rest in the fact that I am here to take care of her.*

He continued: "Nadia is trying to overcome her fears. One way she does it is that she makes me the little sister in our play, and she is just brutal to me. She leaves me home at night in the dark, sells off all my belongings, even says I'm responsible for killing my mom and dad, which of course are all reflections of questions she is asking herself—*Was I responsible in some way for my father's death?* She works through it all in the play through me."

I thought about how Nadia had never shied away from emotion. She was like a pig rolling around in the mud, slathering it all over herself regardless of the emotion—from grief to elation. I had no doubt that I had started out this way—open, curious, wanting to share—but I slowly cut myself off from these big emotions because

I could not process them on my own and I didn't have a safe place to do so externally. But now I did. I was creating that safe place for the two of us, for our small family. I began to notice that by allowing Nadia to feel her feelings, she was teaching me to do the same. From Michael, I learned the psychological theory behind Nadia's ongoing development, but from Nadia, I got to put the theory into practice. As I watched Nadia express and process her feelings openly and honestly, I tried to do the same with her.

One day as I watched Nadia play quietly on the rug I asked her, "What do you and Michael talk about when you see him?"

"We just play," she said flatly, not looking up at me and continuing her play.

"Do you talk about anything?" I persisted. I was hoping to glean a little insight into who she thought Michael was and what she thought of their time together.

She only scrunched her nose, repeating in an exasperated tone, "Mom, we just play." And that was that. Not only was there never any resistance from Nadia in going to see Michael, we never had the need to label who he was and what she was doing. He wasn't a doctor or a therapist, he was just Michael with whom she had a weekly playdate. In addition to her play therapy, Michael helped Nadia heal in a very specific way. He was roughly my age, a father of two young girls about Nadia's age, and Nadia got to pretend once a week that he was her father, and once a week at the end of each session, she was reminded that he wasn't.

"This gives her heart a chance to break a little every week," he had said to me, "instead of creating this big ideal in her mind that would inevitably crash down on her in the future." That statement made my heart break a little too. But at least I could feel it. My little girl had become the catalyst for me to reconnect with my heart, and in this way, she was my teacher.

Upon landing in Las Vegas, my head was swimming with thoughts about Nadia, and my heart was so full of gratitude to have her as my guide in softening my heart that I was a little disoriented as to what I was doing in Vegas. Without really thinking, I phoned the hospital from the airport and the nurse delicately said to me, "Honey, your father is no longer here. You don't need to come to the hospital anymore." She gave me a number to call so I could give instruction as to which funeral home we wanted his body to be delivered to. *Right, right,* I thought. *Now we talk about him as if he's an object, not a person. His body needs to be delivered. He's just a thing now.* My body was jolted with the memory of sitting in the funeral home looking for poems that could describe the mishmash of emotions swirling inside me after Daniel's death. *Oh, I know where we are now,* I thought. My stomach turned oily, and I steadied myself for what I knew would challenge me emotionally, and even though my knees were shaky, I deliberately chose to walk right into the pain this time.

When I pulled into the driveway of my mother's home, the oily feeling in my stomach grew to such proportions, I had to wait in the car until it subsided. I realized that I was more afraid of facing my mother than dealing with the fact that my father had just died. I remembered how difficult it was for both of us to be around each other after Daniel died and how alone I had felt. I did not want to replay that scene and dug deep for the nascent bit of courage that was growing inside me. I gave myself the same kind of pep talk I always gave Nadia. *Dig deep, Laila. You can do this. You cannot control what your mother does, but you can stay true to who you are.*

Dig deep, dig deep, dig deep, I silently repeated, as I slowly turned the doorknob and entered my mother's home. The house felt empty and the air heavy as I walked through the kitchen. At first, I didn't see my mother. She was curled up with her knees to her chest like a small child, wedged so tightly in the corner of the oversized sofa that the throw pillows billowed around her as if they could pull her in with one swift suck. She had the blanket pulled all the way up to her chin, and if it weren't for her dark hair peeking out, I would have missed her altogether. She was so small as to be invisible.

"Hi, Momma." I put my bag down and went to her. She looked lost, her eyes vacuous and unable to focus. I sat on the edge of the sofa and searched for her hand under the blanket, trying to make eye contact with her. "How are you doing?" I asked as gently as I could.

All she could do was look at me, but really it felt like she was looking through me. "He's gone. They called me this morning and told me when he died."

"Yes, I know. I'm sorry."

"I didn't go see him. I couldn't."

I froze. I did not know what to say to this. I was mad at her for not being strong enough to be with him, but even in that moment, I realized I was also mad at myself for not moving more quickly. I chose to be kind, knowing she couldn't handle any sort of admonishment from me and believing that guilt was enough punishment for inaction—hers, as well as mine. All I could think to say that was honest and balanced was, "Yes, it's very sad that we weren't there with him."

She nodded her head, reached for her cigarettes, and looked out the window. That was my cue that the conversation was over. I got up to go into the back bedroom to unpack and start making phone calls to make arrangements for my father's funeral. Sitting on the edge of my mother's bed, I felt a heaviness envelope me like a thick blanket. *My father is gone*, I thought, the finality of his passing starting to register. I would never be able to say anything to him again. In that moment, I also realized that even though my mother was alive and only about ten feet away from me, she felt as distant as my father. Here we were, two women related to each other, who had lost their husbands in less than two years, yet we were as far apart as ever. I started to feel a familiar anger rise up within me, the one that demanded my mother step up, but I also heard a small voice in my head saying, "It takes two to tango," which shifted my anger back toward me and turned it into shame. I knew I couldn't be mad at her this time around because I more fully understood what was happening. She was trying to stay away from her emotions by numbing out—trying not to feel the pain—which was exactly what I had always done too. And even though I had been working on allowing myself to feel, my knee-jerk reaction was still, *Oh, okay, you don't want to talk about this; I'll just go into the bedroom and work on making funeral arrangements.* It gave me something to do and it's what I did well—infinitely easier than sitting with my mom with all the uncomfortable, unspoken emotions swimming between us. I saw how complicit I was in my mother's inability to connect with me, because I too was still learning how to be brave enough to stay in all that pain. I may have wanted it intellectually, but I wasn't yet fully there emotionally.

I shifted my weight on the bed as a way to throw off the heavy blanket of sadness pressing down upon me. *Fair enough*, I thought, *but I'm committed to keep trying.* The last year and a half had proven to me that showing the tiniest bit of vulnerability had not resulted in my falling apart. Despite my fear, I had been leaning into the resistance and had made my way through the emotional ups and downs and dark moments in my life. And even though being sad and despondent was not my favorite thing, it wasn't as bad as I had made it out to be. It certainly wasn't worth contorting myself to avoid those feelings and cutting off my emotional vitality in the process. In fact, I had experienced instances of light that made me feel more alive than I had in a long time. Here was life giving me another chance to be open and authentic in the face of loss. This time I knew that putting on a strong face and pretending everything was all right was not going to leave me in a better place afterwards. I now knew the price I had been paying for numbing out, and I only had to look at my mother to see where that road would lead. Rather than be angry at my mother's inability to be emotionally more present, I vowed to try my best to stay with whatever feelings arose in me despite what my family did.

I opened my computer and created a folder called Eulogies. I dragged all of the files from Daniel's ceremony in there and opened up a new document entitled Dad's Eulogy. I picked up the phone to call my friend Dana who had helped me think through Daniel's eulogy, and the two of us commented on how we had to stop meeting this way. She asked me questions about my dad and got me to think more broadly about him as a person. In very little time, I had captured enough ideas to write something that was a balanced and positive reflection on my father.

Over the next couple of days, I busied myself with planning my dad's service, finished writing the eulogy, collected old photos of my father, and created a visual montage of my father's life. I found a contemporary jazz arrangement of a beautiful old song by Fairuz, the famous Lebanese singer, to play during the montage. There was something about the combination of the quintessentially Lebanese voice of Fairuz accompanied by a more Western sound that seemed to capture my father's journey from Beirut to Las Vegas perfectly. The day of my father's service, I drove my mother to the chapel. In the distance, I saw three handsome older men wearing double-breasted suits standing outside of the funeral home. They could have come straight out of a 1970s Las Vegas mafia movie like *Casino* or *Goodfellas*. I smiled, feeling proud of the fact that my father belonged to this tribe during that era. I parked my car and laced my arm into the crook of my mother's as we walked into the foyer. Oddly enough, comforting her made me feel better too.

The slideshow I had created was playing on two screens hanging above the doors to the chapel, and the delicate instrumental sounds of the flute, violin, and piano backed by soft percussion beats with the voice of Fairuz wafting over the speakers immediately took you back to my father's Middle Eastern roots. The melody was sad. I could only understand a few words here and there—something about being neighbors with the moon—but I pictured people in the old country hanging out on their balconies chatting with their neighbors and looking up at the moon. My mother looked up at me, surprised, then smiled gratefully for what I had done. We passed people I didn't know pausing before the slideshow, smiling with wet eyes, and whispering amongst each other as the random assortment of pictures cycled through.

I took my mother to the front of the chapel and stood in front of my father's open casket. *Still handsome*, I thought. I left my mother with my uncle and other family members, and I went back to make sure everything was in place. There were many people I did not know. As my father had never shared his personal life with us, I never really knew who he was as a person outside of our home, and this thought made me so very sad. I found a seat toward the back and waited for people to settle in. I felt a tap on my shoulder from the person in the pew behind me.

"Excuse me, are you George's daughter?" A nice-looking, casually dressed man with gray hair and kind blue eyes looked back at me.

"Yes, I'm Laila," I responded, grateful to engage with someone.

"I thought that was you. I recognize you from your pictures. I'm Bobby Stamper. I worked with your father at the Sands in the early seventies. Do you know how proud your father was of you? He talked about you all the time."

"Oh, that's so nice to hear. My dad told you about me?"

"He never stopped talking about you. How you went away to college and bought a house in San Francisco and how smart you were and how well you were doing in business . . ." His voice trailed off as he looked past me. "I never met a father prouder of his daughter."

An overwhelming urge to cry overtook me. Really? *Really*? I wanted to hug this stranger in that moment. He saw how emotional I got and took out a handkerchief and handed it to me. "Yes, your dad was something all right. Those early days at the Sands were a special time."

I composed myself, wanting to take advantage of the opportunity to hear something about my father and his past that he would never have shared with us. "Please, can you tell me a little about what it was like?"

Bobby smiled and leaned forward toward me, and I reclined against the pew so that our heads were just a few inches apart. "Well, back in those days, the Sands was the high roller house on the Strip. Sinatra and Dino and Sammy Davis Jr. were running around the place and were performing in the Copa Room. It was the place to be seen, and your father and me, we worked in the high roller pit on the high-stakes craps table. George Tarraf, Bobby Stamper, Anthony Cigliani, and Carlos Ravelo. We were like rock stars back then. You know this was before you had to wear a uniform on the Strip. We had to go down to see Doc on Fremont Street, and he would tailor-make your shirts and set you up with a beautiful pair of wing-tipped oxford shoes that were eighty dollars a pair. You know back then, that was a lot of money."

I tried to imagine the scene that Bobby painted. I remember once I overheard my dad telling a friend that the old seventies TV stars Bob Newhart and Suzanne Pleshette used to play at his table all time. I didn't realize that the Rat Pack had filmed *Ocean's 11* there in the sixties, putting the Sands on the map and making it a destination for high rollers, celebrities, and mafia bosses alike. And my dad was right in the middle of all that.

"And you know," Bobby said, "there was no real casino marketing back then. We were the juice, and we were responsible for bringing in and creating an experience for the high rollers that brought them back again and again. I'm sure you know, your father being as handsome as he was, he could really bring in the ladies . . ."

I smiled, as this had been the ongoing theme throughout my father's life. How handsome he was, what a ladies' man he was, how girls would follow him around from Beirut to Las Vegas. It was his brand and he wore it proudly. Looking back at Bobby, I could tell he had been just as handsome as my father was, and I assumed the other two guys on the crew probably rounded out the old-school Las Vegas version of a boy band. Bobby just kept on talking, and as he did, I felt myself holding on to every word.

"And not only did we have a ball," Bobby said, "we made a lot of money too! Back then there weren't many guys that could run a craps table the way we did. There weren't many guys that had the skill our crew had; it was early days. Your dad had been dealing in Lebanon, and Carlos came from Cuba and really taught us the game."

I remember my dad laying out the green felt of the craps table at home with all its markings and people coming over and learning how to play the game. He never allowed the kids to watch, quickly sending us to our rooms when his friends came over. Consequently, I never knew how good he was.

"Your father was like a human computer," Bobby said. "He held all the odd combinations in his head, and he was fast. Very impressive. And back then, if the Sheik from Oman plopped down a ten-thousand-dollar tip, the crew split it amongst ourselves, and remember—this was before tips were taxed. Ah, the good old days . . ." His voice trailed off.

This resonated with me because my father put three kids through private school on a dealer's salary back in the seventies. The good ol' days indeed. Bobby continued to speak, sharing the broader history of Las Vegas with me, how the gaming commission was set up in 1959, how Vegas attracted the mafia from Cuba and other parts of the country, and how over time the corporations took it over so that the Vegas he knew disappeared altogether. I realized it really was a very special time and place, and my father had played a starring role in it. It must have been what fed his soul, or rather his ego, as he certainly didn't get that kind of attention at home. All my memories of our family centered around my parents' big fights, and I was always the mediator and ultimately, my mom's protector. The disconnect between the two realities made me want to scream.

As the service began, I made my way back up to the front of the chapel. A few of my father's friends and his cousin got up to say a few words about him, and my brother and I looked at each other as if to say, *Who are they talking about?* We did not recognize the man they were describing in these stories—funny, a good friend, a teacher, and a mentor. Regret flooded through me anew with each vignette that was shared about my father. One young Turkish man in his thirties pulled me aside after the service and went on and on about how my dad was more of a father to him than his own father ever had been. He also told me about how much my father talked about me and how proud he was of me.

When it was time for me to read the eulogy, I was full of so much love and pride for my father, and so much regret that I had missed a huge side of him, that I immediately burst into tears as I started to read. I tried to soldier on, when I felt an arm around my shoulder. I almost jumped at the very touch of someone trying to comfort me. I looked up and saw my uncle Robert, my mother's brother, looking down and nodding but holding me tight. It was initially disorienting, but almost instantly I realized that this was what it felt like to be held, literally and figuratively, in your moment of need.

Thank you, I mouthed to my uncle. I sputtered through the end of my piece and sat down next to my mom, her head hung low, her eyes looking at her fingertips. Instead of feeling hurt or angry as I did after Daniel had died, I could only feel deep compassion for her in that moment. A light bulb went off in my head right then and there. First, my mom wasn't withholding anything from me; it wasn't that she refused to comfort me but that she just didn't know how to do it. She had spent her entire life numbing her pain in one way or another as a defense mechanism, and I could hardly blame her. And two, the apple didn't fall too far from the tree.

Leaving my mother a few days later was exceptionally difficult. When I went to hug her goodbye, I thought that she held on to me just a few seconds longer than she normally did. As I started to melt into her embrace, she pulled away and said softly, "Thank you for all you did here, honey."

"Of course, Momma," I responded. What was unspoken for us in that moment was that this was her way of saying she loved me.

Rather than feeling irritated that I was only valued for what I could do, I was able to interpret the hidden meaning in those words: *I'm not good at showing my emotions, but I want you to know I really appreciate and love you.* I no longer felt the need to have her say exactly what I wanted. I could see she loved me, and I knew that we were both hurting in our own ways.

"Please call me if you need anything, okay, Mom?"

And with that, I threw my bags in the rental car and made my way to the airport. As I boarded my flight back to San Francisco, I was emotionally spent but felt a calm come over me. My father's death had helped me tease out the truth from the narrative I had been working from my whole life, which brought me great relief. The first was that even though my mother and father were both emotionally stunted, there was no doubt that they both loved me. At the same time, I experienced the power of being seen and held by my uncle and realized how basic a need that is for all humans. For the first time in my life, I allowed myself to feel the pain associated with not having this as I grew up, and I was also able to stay with the sadness and pain associated with my father's death on a much deeper level than I had with Daniel's death. I didn't hide from my pain, and I experienced firsthand how it didn't weaken me but actually made me feel stronger. I started to recognize that in relationships, we are more powerful when we are vulnerable, and I had nothing to fear.

I began to wonder if I would be able to have a deeper relationship with my mom in the years we had left together. *I have to try*, I thought. *I can't wait for her to change or to reach out to me. It has to be me.* And for the first time, I was actually okay with that.

———

The summer ended without fanfare. I continued to try to convince Pat that we needed to revisit the guiding principles he had articulated nearly eight years earlier at Peet's, but he wasn't having any part of it yet. I checked in on my mom weekly by phone. While most conversations were superficial, there were a few where she showed some emotion, and I quickly reciprocated when I saw there was an opening. That fall, Nadia entered kindergarten at the French American International School—I'd finally had my interview and had decided this was the right place. As I dropped her off at school in her red-and-white polka dot dress, with only French-speaking teachers all around us, my tears welled up with a mix of emotions most parents feel in dropping their babies off on the first day of kindergarten. Mine was also tinged with a sad realization that this would be one of many future rites of passage that I wouldn't be able to share with her father, and it reminded me anew just how young Daniel had died and how many of these life moments we would all miss as a family together.

CHAPTER 10

DEVELOPING THE BODY OF A COACH

"It takes courage to grow up and be who you really are."
—E.E. CUMMINGS

At work, we were slowly making our way out of the "Great Recession," and it started to feel like we could expand our focus beyond cutting costs and "driving operational efficiencies." More and more, my team began planning ways we could invest in and support our employees as they grew in their careers at Peet's. We rolled out a competency model giving greater visibility to the skills and capabilities that were expected at each stage of growth, from individual contributors to senior leaders, and subsequently built out a broad training curriculum that taught all new hires everything from how to brew the perfect cup of coffee or tea to how to give open and honest feedback during a performance conversation. I saw how most managers avoided what they viewed as the hard conversations, and I found myself coaching them on how to have these discussions in a direct yet compassionate manner. I soon realized that, for me, sifting through the best options and determining the optimal strategy in approaching a difficult conversation was infinitely easier than actually sitting down with someone and being present with the difficult emotions that arose. Of course, I thought, this is why we all avoid "hard conversations," because to do them right, you have to be fully present and allow yourself to feel what's coming up for you and for the person with whom you're speaking. This brought me face-to-face with my most vulnerable self—this new self that wasn't just focused on getting tasks done but was also learning how to feel my own emotions and those of others.

For years, when people would leave my office after a meeting, they would ask, "Open or closed?" as they held the door lever in their hands. My standard response was always, "Closed, you know I don't like people," after which I would give a little smile and go back to my work. I knew this comment made them uneasy, an inadvertent Freudian slip revealing the battle going on inside of me. Of course, I cared for my people. I regularly went into battle for them, and I knew they recognized this. But I also had an off switch, emotionally speaking, where I would go dark if I felt people were getting too "whiny." But following my father's death, my tolerance for what I would have previously judged as "emotional neediness" began to increase. Very, very slowly, I was allowing a little more feeling into my work. I forced myself to stay in the hard conversations a little longer every time, and the more I did it, the braver I became and the more skillful at navigating through them. It was like threading a needle between courage and compassion. Over time, I noticed that my ability to withstand the emotional heat strengthened my heart muscle, which increased my compassion.

I felt like a drill sergeant starting to soften, but I didn't want the troops to think that I was some kind of pushover. I still held this belief that strength and vulnerability—aka weakness—were on opposite ends of the spectrum, on a seesaw of sorts. I worried that if I traveled too far away from strength toward vulnerability, the balance would shift, and I would slide into vulnerability, becoming exactly the kind of person I had always rolled my eyes at and silently judged. So, while I would allow myself to show moments of tenderness here and there, I maintained a firm hold on the strong side of the seesaw for fear of losing my power.

One day, as I was sitting in my office looking up at my over-sized whiteboard covered with ink from previous brainstorming sessions, I noticed a quote high up and to the right: *Less Talk, More Action,* in big blue letters. I was in the habit of pointing to this phrase when I felt that people were going down a rabbit hole, overthinking things, or, if I'm being honest, felt like they were wasting my time with nonsensical rambling. *How long had I had that up there as my calling card?* I suddenly realized that it was no longer what I wanted to be known for. I found myself picking up an eraser and trying to erase the phrase, but it had been up there so long, the ink would not fade. I grabbed the spray bottle and a few paper towels to try again. As I scrubbed away at each letter on the board, it felt like I was simultaneously erasing them from my mind as well—from my narrative, the one that drove me to keep moving. I smiled as I saw the connection between what I was doing externally and what was happening inside of me. *Takes a lot of effort to erase those long-held beliefs.* I leaned in harder and put some muscle into removing the dark blue ink until the letters disappeared completely, leaving nothing but a shiny whiteboard.

As I allowed myself to feel more, things in all areas of my life began to unfold. I found myself wanting to do more yoga instead of my high-intensity workouts. I stopped going to Bikram hot yoga—which was a more intense, physically punishing workout—and started going to a new kind of yoga class called Anusara. Anusara yoga was focused more on gentle, heart-opening poses, and over time, my weekly yoga classes unwittingly became my spiritual practice.

I became a regular at Darcy Lyons's class in Hayes Valley every Saturday at 11 a.m. Darcy was a dancer and a therapist and had a way of weaving a specific intention at the beginning of class with what went through your head during the class. One day she had us pay special attention to our "edge," that imaginary line that, when crossed, would result in pain and discomfort, either physical or mental.

"Notice how your body reacts when you push against your edge. Does it tighten up and resist? What could happen if you allowed yourself to breathe into that space..." She was always trying to get us to recognize when we were holding our breath and how to use breath as a way to move through our discomfort and open up new channels.

On this day in particular, I was really struggling with my poses. My sense of balance was off, and my inner critic was on full volume. *Geez, Laila, what is your problem? Get it together, you look ridiculous. You should be so much better at this point; you've been doing this for months!* Seething with inadequacy, I spied a lovely young yogini holding the pose masterfully next to me, and just as my inner critic started to berate me anew, I heard Darcy say, "Just remember, we all have an edge, and while it may look different in each one of us, *the suffering feels exactly the same inside. The suffering feels the same, no matter what it looks like on the outside.*" That really hit home with me, and in an instant, a rush of self-compassion came over me such as I had never felt before. In that moment, I realized how ridiculous it was to make these superficial external comparisons. Suffering is suffering, pain is pain, regardless of its origin, and regardless of how it looks from the outside. Instead of envy or jealousy or judgment, in that moment all I felt was compassion for myself and empathy for others. It was so much harder to judge others when I realized that my pain was theirs too.

In another class with Diego del Sol, as I lay down in savasana at the end of a deep yoga class, Diego encouraged us to go into our hearts. This was the kind of exercise I used to disdain, thinking it was a waste of time, but that day, I tried. I imagined my heart to be a flower—a rosebud—but it was completely closed and clenched up. At first, I wasn't sure if my bud was even alive, but as I started working through my meditation, a warm yellow-white glow began to emanate from my bud, and suddenly one petal began to unstick and peel away. The glow intensified, and as the first thin petal peeled back, I noticed there was another delicate petal attached to it, and it began to peel back as well, only to reveal a connection to a third, and a fourth and a fifth. I stayed with my flower, allowing it to open as the warm circle of light around it grew and grew. The light was pure energy coming from the flower, and as it opened, the light intensified. Physically, I felt like I was opening too, and I relaxed my shoulders to make more space for my opening. Now the rosebud had transformed into a beautiful rose with a multitude of velvety red petals fanning out in a spiral from the center. The glow had become a golden halo around the flower and encircled my whole torso.

Diego encouraged us to go further and to try to see what was at the center of our hearts. "Who is your inner master?" he asked. The rose was so completely open now that I could see a pure white light starting to peek out of the center. I went into my flower, into the center, and as the last petal gave way, the pinprick of white light broke open and flooded my entire body. It shot out of my legs and feet and arms and the top of my head. It was blinding and all-encompassing, and it held me in a space that felt safe and contented. At the very origin of this light, I could vaguely see a tiny figure. A little baby Buddha waving and laughing up at me. I started to silently cry. I always thought I was so tough, I never expected to see this at my core. I understood so deeply in that moment that all my survival mechanisms had started as a way to protect my baby Buddha, but this was what was at my core and who I was in my very essence—a beautiful, innocent light-being, full of love and compassion. I held on to that feeling for a very long time that day, and I was able to go back into that space in future meditations. It always felt like coming home and had the ability to ground me when I started to feel unhinged.

There were many yoga classes where I would erupt into tears without really knowing why. I was embarrassed at first, trying to hide my tears, but after a while I realized that whatever was happening for me on the mat was not something I could control and that there was something deeper happening that I just had to allow. I started to see how out of balance I had become—big head, little heart, and virtually no body connection. My yoga practice began to break down the walls I had erected that separated me from all the negative emotions I wouldn't allow myself to feel in the moment they arose and to the wisdom I had in my body all along. There was a lot to work through. Week after week, I tapped into some element of rage or fury or sadness that had been unexpressed for decades while I hid behind my nice, pleasing outer facade. It had always been so difficult for me to show anger, but I knew I had to go there to reclaim all the parts of me. I didn't really understand what I was doing but felt compelled to continue to explore everything within and allow myself to peel back layers of unexpressed emotions that had calcified over my heart. I truly understood the statement that feelings that are not acknowledged do not go away; they go underground and bind us to the past.

My fear of losing myself in my emotions was balanced by some indescribable pull to go deeper into my heart. It was as if there was a battle going on inside of me, a tug of war between my head and my heart, and for the first time in my life, my heart had a little more agency, or maybe it was that my head didn't hold on so tightly to its position. Whatever the reason, I felt myself drawn more and more to look within and go further on my personal development path.

Around this time, I was invited by a leadership coach I had been introduced to through my work to be part of a weekend workshop for female executives. I didn't know much about it except that there would be about eight of us and we would spend the weekend getting to know ourselves and each other better. We met at the apartment of one of the coaches in Cole Valley, dug deep into our narratives, questioned our limiting beliefs, and created vision boards about what we wanted in our lives. We also did exercises that were simple yet powerful in bringing us closer to each other. This required vulnerability and compassion. I felt like a fawn on new legs most of the weekend, but I felt safe enough to go outside of my comfort zone. When the weekend was over, I was emotionally spent but hooked. I didn't know what this was, but I wanted more of it. It awoke something deep inside me, and I yearned for more—more connection, more authenticity in connection, more truth in connection.

At work, I was telling Pat about my weekend, aware of just how "woo-woo" the words sounded as they came out of my mouth. I saw a smile creep out of the corner of his mouth.

"What?" I asked, suddenly feeling self-conscious, retreating into my shell.

"I'm not really sure what you're talking about, but whatever it is you're doing, it's working for you. You should continue to pursue it."

I wasn't sure what he meant by that, but his supportive comment gave me the courage to ask him if the company could support me in this effort.

"Oh great," I responded. "Hey, do you think that Peet's would consider supporting me in getting my coaching certification? It would take me away from work every quarter for a few days, but I will make sure nothing gets dropped . . ."

"I think we could probably do that," he said with a smile.

"Thanks, Pat. I really appreciate it." I left his office and signed up, diving headfirst into an intense coaching program alongside nineteen other strangers whom I would get to know better than anyone in my life to that point. It was a year of deep, purposeful work examining my lifelong, closely held beliefs. I was an archeologist, exploring and excavating the deep pockets of my mind, tapping into my nascent emotional and somatic intelligence.

The learning came slowly. It was like acquiring a new language. So much of what James, my coaching instructor, said, I barely understood. For example, I learned that in order to be a good coach, you have to develop the "body of a coach." *The body of a coach? What's he talking about?* Eventually I learned that in order to be present with suffering—mine, as well as others'—I had to develop the physical ability to hold that place without trying to hide from the pain.

"The ability to be with someone else's suffering is called compassion," he would say. "And the other person's ability to open up and experience their pain in your presence is tied directly to whether or not they can feel your compassion."

I could understand this, but I wasn't sure how I was going to apply this to my day-to-day work. As if reading my mind, James continued: "Problem-solving is the opposite of compassion. When someone moves straight into problem-solving, the other person feels judged and will not feel safe to open up."

I started to see the problem with the way I had led: I had relied on my intellect too frequently, moved to action too quickly, and didn't allow myself to stay long enough in heart-centered connection with people. On top of that, my natural energy level was intense and always revved up. The combination of my quick mind and my bias for action didn't leave a lot of room for debate, and I realized I was probably missing important information, not to mention the opportunity to connect on a deeper level. I used to worry that if I was "too nice" I couldn't be effective, that I had to maintain a safe emotional distance to maintain my power. What I learned was the deeper I could go within myself, the deeper I could go with others, which gave me a greater capacity and ability to hold the space for difficult conversations. I allowed myself to stay with the negative feelings that came up when I was telling someone they were not performing well or that I had received negative feedback about them. I stayed close to the discomfort and I tried not to judge. The combination of those two things changed the quality of my conversations and my relationships with people. I wasn't being any less direct about what the problem was, I was just able to balance it with kindness and nonjudgmental compassion.

My coaching also helped me be a better mother. I was aware that I didn't want to repeat the patterns of my childhood in my relationship with Nadia. I didn't want her to feel as driven as I had felt, or as responsible. I didn't want her to feel she had to develop a protective outer shell to be successful, and I knew I had to be more present with her feelings than I had been with people at work. I needed to learn a new way.

One lesson James shared with us was about another parent who needed help in finding the right balance between pushing her daughter to achieve while supporting her at the same time. James had offered a shift in how this mother might think about her child. He told her, instead of thinking about your child as a talented athlete that you have to train to prepare for the Olympics, rather think of her as a priceless piece of art and you are an art curator; your only job is to notice and appreciate the subtleties and uniqueness of this beautiful piece of art.

I had been oscillating between athletic coach and art curator, alternately driving and appreciating Nadia her whole life. This metaphor really helped me to temper my "coach" instincts so that I wouldn't end up driving her the way I had been driving myself my whole life. Being able to think about Nadia as a masterpiece rather than raw clay that needed to be molded helped me shift my parenting style tremendously. When I allowed myself to slow down and notice the whole of who Nadia was, I was able to truly see what a masterpiece she already was—the mix of her buoyant energy combined with her delicate sensitivity came together like no other. Like all children, like all people, like me. I got my first taste of what it meant to be imperfectly perfect.

Nadia would regularly say things that reminded me of how connected she was to her feelings and to her instincts—how perfect she was already without my tweaking. I started to call her my Baby Buddha. I recalled her coming home from kindergarten one day, sharing all that had happened that day.

"And then, Mommy, Aidan made me very mad."

"What did you do?" I asked, only half listening.

"Well, whenever I get angry or stressing, I go to the peace rug and I sit crisscross applesauce." I started to tune in a little more now. I loved how she misused some words ("stressing"), enjoying them for as long as possible because she was losing her baby words far too fast for my liking.

"What's the peace rug, honey?"

"It's a rug in class that we can sit on when we need to relax. And Mommy, when I sit crisscross applesauce on the peace rug, and I'm really, really quiet, nature goes on me, instead of me going on nature." She looked up at me with a smile, blinking her big brown eyes as she finished her sentence.

I stared at her, not knowing what to say. *Nature goes on me, instead of me going on nature.* My five-year-old was intuitively aware of when she was receiving and when she was transmitting, when she was allowing and not forcing her will onto others. I thought to myself, *I bow before you, Baby Buddha, my pint-sized teacher.*

But at the same time I was learning from her, I was also teaching her. Nadia was so delicate and so emotional, I found I had to help her self-soothe and build her resilience. The challenge for me was how to build her emotional resilience without crushing her spirit. I couldn't come at her with my direct, take-no-prisoners style. I had to approach her from a place of love and tenderness, which took a lot more effort than demanding something of her from an ungrounded, disconnected place. But I was motivated to do it for my little girl. I don't know if it was my maternal instincts or if I was keenly aware of the opportunity I had in front of me for a do-over in how I had been raised, but I found the patience and the will to keep at it—most of the time. In a way, we were teaching each other reciprocal lessons. She was teaching me how to soften, and I was teaching her to be more resilient.

The more I strengthened my heart, the less I felt I needed to be tough on the outside. There was a shift happening within me. I was moving from being soft and fragile on the inside and tough as nails on the outside to tough and resilient on the inside and softer and more tender on the outside, all the while dropping my hyper-vigilant, defensive posture to the world. The low-grade anxiety that had always been inside me was beginning to recede. I trusted more in the world and in my ability to meet the challenges ahead of me. Who would have thought that real fearlessness is the product of tenderness? Certainly not me, but it was happening ever so slowly within me, which encouraged me to continue on my journey.

As I approached my fourth anniversary at Peet's, the personal and professional came together when I had the chance to go on a coffee-buying trip to Nicaragua. Every year at Peet's, we had sent a group of new hires to Costa Rica so that they could learn the coffee business up close and personal. We wanted to make sure that our employees saw firsthand the business we were in, the relationships we had that had spanned decades with coffee growers, and the kind of impact we were having on developing countries through these long-lasting relationships. We also wanted to remind them that coffee was an agricultural product, we weren't dealing with computer chips or plastic widgets; there was an alchemy, a beautiful dance to growing, picking, milling, drying, and bagging green coffee beans to be shipped all over the world before we roasted them in our manufacturing plant in Alameda, California. Making coffee was a complex, multipart process, and we wanted our key employees to appreciate the origin of our business, far from spreadsheets and board meetings.

Ironically enough, I had missed the trip every single year for one reason or another, so when our coffee buyer, Shirin, asked if I wanted to join her on a trip to Nicaragua, I jumped at the chance, feeling a real need to get closer to the "countries of origin," as we called them. We took a 7 a.m. flight to Miami that connected with a flight to Managua, arriving at 8 p.m. We were picked up by Julio, whose family had owned a number of farms in Nicaragua over the generations. He would be our escort and guide during our few days in the country. We learned that Nicaragua is the poorest Central American country. They dealt with an earthquake in 1972 that decimated its infrastructure, which was followed by the overthrow of the Somoza dictatorship by the Sandinista rebels who governed Nicaragua for over a decade before the U.S.–backed Contras took back the government in 1990. Twenty-eight years of revolutionary war had had a major impact on the country, and there were still men in military fatigues carrying assault rifles everywhere we went. I remembered hearing news reports about the Contras and Sandinistas when I was in school, but it was this thing happening to other people far from me that I never fully understood. Being in Nicaragua, learning about the struggle, and meeting people whose lives had been touched by the war was a whole other story.

On our first day, Julio took us to a farm in Jinotega that was run by a woman named Angelina. We had driven through windy roads full of ditches and protruding tree trunks to arrive at a beautiful, lush forest high in the mountains. Peet's only purchased Arabica beans, which are grown at higher altitudes and are much more flavorful than those grown at lower altitudes. As I got out of the jeep, my insides still felt like they were moving as I tried to get my legs under me. Angelina was an older woman in her late sixties, no more than five feet tall, but with a solidity to her that I noticed straight away. She showed us around the farm and invited us inside for lunch in her modest yet well-kept hacienda.

"My family was not in the coffee business," she said. "I learned it from my father-in-law."

"Is this your family's business, then?" I asked.

"Yes, all four of my children have their own jobs, two are lawyers and two are business managers, but they work the farms on the weekend. I run the farm by myself during the week and keep my twelve grandchildren with me, and they see their parents on the weekend."

Shirin began to ask Angelina about the history of the farm and how she had fared during the revolutionary war. She told us that her kids were too young to fight with the Sandinista rebels, so they were out on countryside farms teaching literacy. She explained that her family did not side with the rebels but rather were conscientious objectors, so the government made them go out and teach, promising they would subsequently pay for their university education.

"In the end, they did not keep their promise," Angelina said, and gave a weak chuckle. "I had to pay for my kids to get educated myself."

"So, you were for the Contras, you supported Somoza?" I asked, trying to determine which side of the conflict she was on.

"I tried to remain neutral during those years. I did what I had to do to keep my farm and my family together."

Shirin and I recalled our conversation with Julio that morning. He'd insisted that everything that had been done for the country was thanks to Somoza and that "*nada nada nada*" was done by the Sandinistas. Sitting with Angelina at her farm, she recounted that while she did not support the Sandinistas, Somoza's regime did nothing—"*nada nada*"—and took all the money for themselves.

"Before, I used to get three flat tires on the road to Jinotega, bringing the coffee in. Now I have to pay for electricity, but at least I *have* electricity and the road to Jinotega is good, at least passable."

I listened to Angelina tell her story without bitterness or anger, and I marveled at her ability to stay strong and centered given everything she had gone through.

"Just recently, I was kidnapped for thirty hours, but thank goodness my daughter paid the fifty-thousand-dollar ransom," she said. She spoke with a mix of disgust and resignation as if to say, *What are you going to do?*

I was shocked at everything she told me. *Kidnapping? Ransom?* "Who, what, why?" I asked.

She smiled, looking at me kindly. "There are still people up in the mountains who are against the government and who stir up trouble like this from time to time."

I thought about how easy my life had been compared to Angelina's. Because of this she had learned the lesson long before me that one cannot control what happens in life. She had learned to do what she could to improve her life and to accept what she could not do. This was completely unlike me, who had clung so completely to the certainty that I could bend things to my will, numbing myself to life's eventual ups and downs in the process. I began to see how Daniel's and my father's sudden deaths had been a gift for me to see this reality. I was an iceberg thawing after years of not allowing

STRONG LIKE WATER

myself to be touched by anything negative. But now in Nicaragua, I was like a leaky faucet, trying to hold back tears as Angelina shared her story with us. Angelina noticed my struggle and excused herself to bring us lunch.

She set a large bowl of oily chicken soup in front of us, and I tried to eat as much as I could, knowing it would be a significant insult if I didn't. I managed to make a dent in it despite the queasiness I felt arising in my stomach. Before we headed off to our next farm I went to hug Angelina goodbye and involuntarily burst into tears. She pulled back and held my hands in her rough, thick palm. With a smile on her face, she tapped my face a few times.

"You have a very tender heart," she whispered to me as she released my face.

As we got into the jeep, Shirin looked at me and asked if I was okay, then offered: "You hear these stories all the time when you're in this business. It makes me feel better about the work I do because I know that by buying their beans, we are helping them in a very real way."

I could only nod as we took off down the bumpy, windy road, so grateful for the experience I was having. The rest of the trip was filled with similar stories of women who had experienced hardship and loss but were always, always filled with gratitude for what little they had and a beautiful combination of strength and tenderness.

I left Nicaragua with a very felt sense of the path I was on. These women were strong and capable to be sure, but they were also kind and tender and compassionate. *I think I've had this whole thing wrong my entire life,* I thought. Maybe there's not a linear spectrum where you are either strong and capable or weak and vulnerable. Maybe, it's more like a DNA strand where the strong and the vulnerable strands weave together, making a strand stronger than one or the other alone. My body started to buzz as I considered this possibility. Life is not a series of either/or choices. Life is both things happening all the time at the same time. It simply requires a change of perspective.

144

A few months later, as I was nearing the end of my coaching program, my instructor James invited a somatic psychologist to come in and lead a session on how it is possible to physically feel discomfort in your own body when coaching someone else. This psychologist had us turn to our partner and take turns coaching each other. Afterwards, she would ask us to call out what we felt in our own bodies as we were listening to what the other person was saying. Hands started to go up in the air, and I heard people saying, "When Adam said he was sad, I felt a tightness in my chest," and, "When Mike talked about his anger, my shoulders raised, and I felt heat go up the back of my neck."

At first, I thought they were making it up, but so many people spoke up, I knew I was missing something. So, my rational mind started searching for reasons why I couldn't feel one thing in my body when it seemed like everyone else could. James must have noticed my expression because he called on me and asked what I was thinking. I didn't know what to say. My mind raced with possible reasons why I couldn't feel anything. Before I knew it, I heard myself say, "Well, I think that I'm such a head person, I don't feel things in my body, and . . ."

James interrupted me and said in front of the entire class, "I quite disagree; I think you're very much a heart person, and your head comes to the rescue of your heart." He said this so quietly and incidentally, I wasn't sure I heard him correctly.

What was he talking about? *My head comes to the rescue of my heart?* As these words sank into my brain, I was overwhelmed with a sadness so strong, I couldn't push it down, and I didn't know why. I had to excuse myself to go to the bathroom, and it took me fifteen minutes to get my wits about me again. What was happening?

I stumbled through the rest of the class and went home that evening still in a daze. I put Nadia to bed and started getting ready for bed myself. As I went through my bedtime routine, I replayed the day, trying to breathe through the tightness in my chest. *My head comes to the rescue of my heart.* I looked at my reflection in the bathroom mirror and a rush of understanding came over me. It wasn't that I was unfeeling and insensitive. It was that I was so sensitive that my head had to come rescue my underdeveloped heart. My overused intellect helped to protect my fragile heart. Seeing it this way shifted my whole self-perception. I wasn't tough. I was gentle, but I had to develop the body of a coach to be able to show my tenderness. I was only tough on the outside; on the inside, I had always been soft. It dawned on me where I was on my journey at that point. As I strengthened my interior, I was simultaneously softening my exterior. There was an inverse relationship between the two. The opposite of what I had always feared was happening. I was softening and getting stronger, not weaker. Softening my heart was not making me soft in the head. How had I had it so wrong for so many years? Simply having someone see me in a way my parents never had, granting me the space to acknowledge my heart for the first time in my life, created a seismic shift in my self-perception. For the first time, I felt like I had permission to be sensitive. I didn't have to lean so hard into my intellect. For me, I knew this realization was a deeply personal one, and hard won.

CHAPTER 11

THE VELVET HAMMER

"We are at our most powerful the moment
we no longer need to be powerful."

—ERIC MICHA'EL LEVENTHAL

D riving to work one day I heard an interview on NPR with an Austrian Benedictine monk named Brother David Steindl-Rast. He was talking about being happy and grateful, and something about the warm evenness in his tone caught my attention. I arrived at work, turned off my engine, and stayed in my car to finish listening to the interview.

"Everything is a gift. The degree to which we are awake to this truth is a measure of our gratefulness, and that gratefulness is a measure of our aliveness," he said, and as I was trying to wrap my head around this statement, I heard him say, "You know the antidote to stress is not necessarily rest."

"What is it then?" the interviewer asked.

"The antidote to stress is wholehearted living."

This statement sank into my consciousness like a sponge quickly absorbing water. It rang deeply true to me, and I immediately made the connection to my journey. Allowing myself to feel both the good *and* the bad while maintaining my agency in life—not falling into a victim mentality—was making me more alive than I ever was when I tried to numb myself to my pain.

Thinking back on how I used to compartmentalize my life as a way to avoid facing what I did not want to confront, it dawned on me: there really is no such thing as work-life balance. We need to bring our whole selves to work, and as I learned to be more heart-centered through coaching and mothering, I became more heart-centered at work. For me, the way this manifested at work was that I became somewhat obsessed with Peet's values. I itched to develop them from the flat, somewhat platitudinal statements about things you should do to something deeper and more holistic, something that would encompass what I had experienced in Nicaragua and really inspire people to think of who they wanted to be. For months I had been bugging Pat about revisiting our values, but he would summarily dismiss me every time I tried to broach the subject. As our annual business kick-off meeting was coming up, I decided to approach him one more time to see if we could do some work on our values.

"They're fine, Laila, leave it alone," he would say. "If it ain't broke, don't fix it."

I'd push back. "Pat, it's been over eight years since you wrote our guiding principles, and our business has changed a ton during that time. We're not the same company we were eight years ago. We've hired lots of new people with vastly different backgrounds, and I really think we need a common set of values that can hold us all together."

"We have them; they're the guiding principles," he would insist.

"I bet you a hundred dollars I couldn't find five people who can articulate what those guiding principles are," I said. Around and around we went, but he continued to resist. Intellectually, I understood why. Peet's culture ran deep, and messing with the guiding principles was akin to performing open-heart surgery. You didn't want to inadvertently hurt the patient. Pat felt it was too high of a risk to take for not a lot of upside. I would let it rest for a few days, but it became clearer to me that we needed a stronger foundation to tie the diversity of our employees and our different channels of business together. It began to feel personal.

One day as I was meeting with Pat on the business kick-off agenda, trying to come up with a meaningful exercise that could forge a connection among the eighty or so attendees, I had an idea.

"Hey, how about we do an exercise where we ask everyone to focus their energy, love, and passion for the company in revisiting our values and making them reflective of who we all are and where our business is today?"

Since he didn't completely shut me down, I kept on talking, extemporaneously throwing ideas out there.

"We can seed the discussion in the fact that a lot has changed over the past few years and we think it's important for us to pause now, refocus on what's important, and commit to the big things that are going to allow us to reach our goals. I mean, we've gone from a local retail business to a multichannel business with national reach. We've grown in revenue, size, and scope. We've hired new people and added new products. Now is the time to do this, right?"

"Right . . ." Pat said. He saw where this was going, but he was coming along so I continued.

"I think it's so important that we give people a voice in this process. That's the Peetly way to do it. I would frame it as something like, 'Given all this change, we thought it would be a good time to take a look at who we are and what we stand for. You shape that every day, and we want to give you a voice in continuing to shape it as we grow.' What do you think?"

Pat smiled and looked down at the sheet of paper in front of him. *He's going to shut me down*, I thought. *He's just thinking about how best to do it now that I'm all amped up.* Pat finally looked up and said, "Okay, but I want to see how this develops every step of the way."

I was stunned but tried to hide it. "Of course. Of course." I couldn't think of anything else to say, and I wanted to get out of his office before he could change his mind. We quickly went through the remaining few items, and I excused myself on the hour, saying I had another meeting waiting for me. As I walked out his office door, he threw me a look and reiterated, "I don't want any surprises on this one, okay?"

"Yep, I understand." I smiled and closed his door, almost skipping back to my office to share the good news with my team. After I conveyed my conversation with Pat to my number two, Kristi, I could see her wheels turning, and I knew she was going to start coming up with some great ideas.

"Give me a few days to think about this and I can show you what I come up with."

"You got it," I told her. We strategically looped Pat in early throughout the process, but by the end, he seemed to lose interest, which meant he thought we were on the right track.

The meeting and the presentation went off without a hitch. It seemed perfectly natural to everyone that we would be taking a look at our values given how much growth the company had experienced, and rather than anyone being alarmed, people gave us feedback that they felt a real responsibility and ownership in making sure we didn't lose what had always made Peet's great while at the same time holding space for what needed to evolve to be more relevant to the business. A few weeks after the meeting, we had taken everyone's feedback and synthesized it down to the big themes that emerged.

We created a cross-functional values committee and began to work with these themes while at the same time looking at the values of other companies. We asked ourselves, which were like us, and which were not? Who did we admire and aspire to be, and who did we not ever want to be? It was like a game of hot and cold, where at first it was easier to know who we were not rather than who we were. We narrowed down the big themes further then took them out on the road. Over a period of sixteen months, we held focus groups, asking employees at all levels in all parts of the organization what felt like Peet's and what didn't, and why. The passion generated in those meetings was electric. People were so into it that we got into seriously heated debates on a variety of subjects. Should we only hire people who were passionate about coffee, or was it okay to hire passionate people in general and trust that their passion would then extend to coffee and tea? Should we consider profitability as one of our values, or would that turn us into capitalistic heathens and destroy everything we'd built? It was a labor of love and everyone took it very, very seriously. From an HR perspective, you couldn't pay for this kind of engagement. People cared so much about the place they worked and felt a personal responsibility to get these values right. We were working at the intersection of heart and impact, and I was in heaven. I realized that this was the workplace manifestation of the personal journey I had been on—bringing the head and heart together to make a greater impact than either could on its own. I was bringing my whole self to work, and life was reciprocating by bringing me deep joy and satisfaction through my work. I was learning to live wholeheartedly just as I heard Brother David suggest. It was all becoming aligned for me.

Over time we whittled down our big seven themes to four values that we felt balanced who we were and what we aspired to be: Mastery, Curiosity, Responsibility, Prosperity. We noticed there was a symbiotic relationship between mastery and curiosity that captured the idea of "the beginner's mind" in Zen Buddhism. This was a challenging concept for dyed-in-the-wool Peetniks: to be a master of our craft, to strive for excellence, yet at the same time, to stay open, challenge the status quo, and discover new possibilities. I had been told when I first joined Peet's that only three master coffee makers' palettes could discern "good" coffee at Peet's, and I saw this limited mindset have a negative effect on our ability to grow and be more relevant in the market. Presenting the idea of curiosity introduced an aspirational element that complemented a culture that strove for perfection in every cup. Likewise, adding prosperity to our values did not immediately feel like Peet's—too corporate, too capitalistic, some said. But we took our time and worked through a definition of prosperity that captured the principle of abundance for everyone in the Peet's ecosystem—from our employees as we offered them exciting growth career opportunities to our local and global communities as we partnered with them to build thriving communities and fulfilling lives. If Peet's the company prospered, so did Angelina in Nicaragua because we bought more beans from her, and so did the barista who worked part-time in Harvard Square during school.

Over the next year, we rolled out a robust onboarding program where we created a book we called Peet's Passions and gave it to each new hire. The book told our story and went into detail about our values and how they showed up in our everyday work. We created a board game that moved people through the squares when they could successfully answer questions they'd learned in their new hire orientation. The whole concept behind Peet's Passions was that we wanted everyone to show us who they really were. We didn't want anyone to feel like they could only show us one side of themselves, like they had to be on their best behavior. "We want you to bring your whole self to work," I told them. "We want to know all of you, not just the professional you." Every quarter at the end of my new hire orientation presentation, I would lead an exercise that we had created and included at the end of our Peet's Passions book that asked people to share what they were passionate about. We had created multicolor stickers that said, "King of" or "Queen of," and others that said things like "gardening" or "motorcycles." We had blank ones so people could fill in whatever it was they were passionate about. We provided everyone with an oversized thick sheet of paper that they ripped out of their books to place these stickers on, and we encouraged them to hang it up in their cubes and offices. Soon, these posters became a way for employees to really get to know each other and discover common interests. It felt good to bring people together in this way.

Soon after we rolled out the values, a request came in to have Pat present at the Haas School of Business Berkeley Entrepreneurs Forum. They wanted two well-known local food companies to discuss the challenges encountered, and lessons learned as they grew. John Foraker, the CEO of Annie's Organics, was one of the speakers, and they wanted Pat to be the other.

Pat turned to me and said, "Why don't you do this? You can present on all the great work you've done with the values."

My jaw dropped to the floor. "Me?" Fear flooded my body, and all I could do in the moment was shake my head no. Speaking in front of over three hundred people alongside another company's CEO? I couldn't fathom it.

Pat smiled. "Why not, Laila? You've been telling the story internally for the past year and a half. You're perfectly suited to do it, and it's at your alma mater. What could be more perfect? Think about it . . ." And with that, he walked off, leaving me alone to internally debate the idea. It didn't take long to realize that he was right, and I was just scared to put myself out there. Eventually, I knew I had to do it, if not for my own professional growth, then to tell the Peet's story, one of which I was so proud.

I worked hard on the presentation and was so nervous the night of the event, I felt nauseous. John Foraker presented first, and he was very good. He gave an engaging business presentation on Annie's, which only served to make me feel like more of a fraud. As I walked up to the podium, looking out at a sea of smiling faces, my butterflies were so strong I could hardly breathe. I put my papers on top of the podium and adjusted the microphone.

"Hello, my name is Laila Tarraf. I'm the chief people officer at Peet's Coffee and Tea, and I'm delighted to be speaking to you tonight." Each time I looked up at the three hundred attendees, my stomach would jump, and I was aware that my voice would drop in volume. Just then I spied an older woman who was smiling warmly at me, and she gave me just enough courage to dig deep and breathe through my butterflies. I continued:

"A lot of the conversations we have at Peet's have to do with how we balance profitability and quality. How we grow with integrity. For us, quality leads to profitability because that's what our brand is built on, but those are not always easy decisions to make." I scanned the room and saw that people were engaged and my friend on the left side of the room was still smiling at me, which gave me even more confidence.

"What do you say to your shareholders when a decision is made that will cost a million dollars that doesn't have an ROI but is consistent with our values? The most valuable asset we have, by far, is the Peet's brand and the company's reputation. The 'brand' is, by definition, what it stands for—its values—in the minds of our customers and our employees. Every opportunity we have—to grow, expand, successfully open new stores, or introduce new products—we have because our customers and our employees believe in, trust, and identify with our brand and our values.

"So, the hard question isn't whether to make a one-million-dollar investment in our brand—the tree that bears all fruit—despite the fact that a traditional ROI may not be calculable. That answer is easy—to not do so could put our most valuable asset—the one that took forty-four years to build—at risk. The harder question is *which* million-dollar investments to make that are consistent with the brand's values, *and when to make them*, because there are so many you could make, and resources are finite.

"Implicit in each decision we make is the question: Do we stay true to our founding principles and potentially limit our growth potential? Do we make choices that enable us to grow but could change who we are fundamentally, and what we've always believed in when it comes to coffee and how we do business—as many others before us have? Or is there a way to sustain our values, what we believe in, and make *that* the engine that enables our growth instead? This is our challenge. To stay true to our founding values and grow profitably. This is the delicate balance that if you're lucky as an entrepreneur you have an opportunity to master in order to grow. Many companies have sacrificed one for the other. I'm going to show you how we have tried to harness our heritage and coffee religion and embed it into our business—in our standards and practices and our systems and processes."

I scanned the room once more and noticed my smiling friend had started to nod in agreement. I smiled back at her and finished my opening remarks before I launched into the values presentation that I knew like the back of my hand because I had been giving it all year. I finished my presentation by saying:

"At Peet's, yes, we believe it's important to know who you are and make the business decisions that are consistent with that. But for us the key to staying true as we grow comes down to how that's translated through our people every day in every moment we have with the customer. We strive to have our people be the physical embodiment of our company, our brand and your values, touching our customers every day with the same message. I know it's a lofty goal, and it's never perfect because we're all human, but staying focused on getting it right hopefully gets us closer every day."

A warmth ran through me as I gathered my notes and the room erupted in applause. I was buzzing with excitement. After a brief panel discussion alongside John Foraker and a moderator from the Haas School of Business, attendees came up to us to ask more questions and to share stories about the first time they discovered Peet's Coffee. Some older attendees even remembered buying their coffee beans from Alfred Peet himself at the corner of Vine and Walnut in the late 1960s. It was a Berkeley lovefest, and I couldn't have been prouder to represent Peet's that night.

News of my presentation had spread back to the office, and work felt so effortless for a few days until one meeting I had with Shawn, my COO, when we really got into it, openly disagreeing on how to handle a challenging performance issue. I didn't feel like he was listening to me, and I'm sure he felt the same. We left the meeting without coming to an agreement on a path forward, and I was wondering if I had pushed too hard. *He probably thinks I'm such a bitch*, I thought to myself as I walked back to my office feeling deflated and annoyed. The next morning, I saw Shawn in the hallway and we both nodded politely to each other, still feeling awkward from the exchange we had the day before. As I settled into my chair and booted up my computer, he opened my office door with a grin on his face and handed me one of the peer recognition cards we had rolled out as part of our employee recognition program that highlighted our values. I looked at the card that had our value of curiosity on it, illustrated with a picture of Albert Einstein sticking out his tongue. I turned it over and saw he had written, "Thank you for always challenging me to be better. While it doesn't always feel good to be on the opposite side of the table from you, I appreciate you caring enough to push me to get to a better outcome." I looked up at him, my mouth open, not knowing what to say. He had a grin on his face and a gleam in his eye waiting for my response.

"Thank you, Shawn. I don't know what to say. You really feel this way?"

"I do. I know it can be hard to push me, and I appreciate it when someone has the courage to do it. You know what people are starting to say about you, right?

"Uh, no, what are people saying?"

"They're calling you the velvet hammer. You've always been tough, but lately you've been able to say things in a way that lets people hear it better. I don't know how to describe it. The words are direct and to the point, but somehow when you deliver them, you get away with it."

I laughed, immediately realizing the velvet hammer metaphor was my finding the right mix of courage and compassion that was allowing me to lead from a place of strength and love. There was no way I was going to say that out loud though; he would have rolled his eyes and walked out the door, so I simply thanked him and told him I'd make sure to stay on him, for his own good, of course.

"Of course," he repeated, and walked out of my office.

I took out a tack from my drawer and pinned the card up on my board, and it stayed there for the next two years as a reminder of the journey I was on.

I was on the same journey to the heart at home.

One night, after dinner as I was helping Nadia get ready for bed, she looked at me with her big brown eyes, brushing away the hair that had gotten into her face from the nightie I had just pulled over her head, and said, "Mom, when you have a heart attack, do you die or do you just stop loving?"

Whaaa? I didn't know quite how to respond at first. Finally, I just said, "Well, neither. You can always choose to love, and hopefully, if it's not a bad heart attack, the doctor can help fix you and you won't die."

She climbed into bed seemingly satisfied with this answer, leaving me to wonder what was going on in that little head of hers. I realized it had been some time since I had touched base with Michael, her therapist, and I e-mailed him that night to make an appointment to see him that week.

As I walked up the stairs in his Pacific Heights walk-up, I saw Michael walking another little boy out of his office before he turned his attention to me. I plopped into my chair and took out my computer so I could take notes during our session.

He sat down into his chair with a smile on his face, but his eyes softened as he began to speak. "I'm so sad," he said, "because I think Nadia is ready to leave."

"Leave? What do you mean, leave, you mean stop seeing you?" I looked up from my computer and saw him nodding.

"I've seen a dramatic change in her play," he said. "She has stopped the disturbing play where she was feeling really toxic, and a lot of her play had to do with really bad people who were going to kick her out or lock her in a cage."

My heart twisted in pain as he described in detail how Nadia had worked through her internal pain through her play with Michael. I tuned in to what he was saying and continued typing.

"Recently, she has introduced a new character into our play. Pinkie Pie exists now, which is a sweet friend Nadia has made up. Nadia usually kills her by the end of our session, but at least she exists. We need to increase her identification with that good girl. There's a part of Nadia that wants to be tough like some of the mean girls at school, but also a part of her that wants to be Pinkie Pie."

Just like me, I thought. "How does this usually play out during your sessions?" I asked, fascinated and hoping I could pick up some parenting pointers I could use.

"Nadia likes to pretend that we are sisters. Nadia plays the fantasy sister who represents her hopes, and she makes me the younger sister and I play her fears. In the play, the sisters' parents have died, and Nadia sells all of my toys while she goes on these fabulous trips without the little sister. I play an unprotected child who hears noises, and Nadia comes back and makes me a meal but then is angry I'm not able to be strong. You see, she wants me to know how it feels to be unprotected. Nadia has had exposure to death, so she can 'see' things because of this."

"I don't even know what to say," I stammered.

"Nadia is a genius in how she uses play to work through her feelings." Michael shook his head in wonderment as he said this.

"Nadia's emotional state is getting more balanced and relaxed. You know a kid is ready to be done with therapy when a transference is resolved. Now I'm Michael, or if we are playing, we can break away from the play, whereas before, if I tried to break from the play to make a connection or ask a question, she would say, 'Just play!' Now, she'll break and want to know more about me because she's less needy to have me be the player in her story. Before, she needed the story to be able to express what she was feeling, and now the feelings are not as big so she can talk about them more directly without having to rely on the play to do it. A year ago, she used to want to sit on my head, lick my face, and be very physical with me. The other day I was going to pick her up and she said,

'Excuse me,' and I thought, *Wow, that's totally appropriate for an eight-year-old girl to say. She should have these boundaries.*

I was typing fast and furiously, not wanting to miss a syllable of what Michael was conveying. When I finished, I looked up and saw that Michael had tears in his eyes, and it dawned on me how hard it must be for him to say goodbye to the kids he grew so close to who then had to leave his practice.

"I don't know how to thank you enough, Michael," I said. "You have been such an amazing part of all our lives, and I'm so grateful for the work you have done with Nadia, me, and Marci!" I gave him a big hug as I left his office and walked out onto Sacramento Street and took in the crisp air around me. I had not realized that Nadia and I had been on parallel paths of sorts. "Her emotional state is getting more balanced and relaxed." *Is that the journey for all of us?* I wondered. I thought about how my work had more meaning, and how I felt more connected to myself, my daughter, and my work of late. Finally, life seemed a little easier; I could breathe more easily. We had found our rhythm, and while I thought of Daniel and my father often, I was at peace and didn't feel their loss as acutely. That would be short-lived, however, as I would soon have a third death to test my new way of being in the world.

CHAPTER 12

FALLING INTO FORGIVENESS

*"Our mothers have been sitting in the dark. Often they choose
this obscurity because their female vision of life is one that they
themselves devalue. We daughters are left feeling motherless because
our mothers have no words to express the depth of their experiences,
and no feminine authority with which to value their lives."*
—NAOMI RUTH LOWINSKY

At Christmas that year, I noticed that my mother's energy was very low, and while she enjoyed watching Nadia and the other grandchildren playing, she appeared to be retreating more and more into herself. I felt that something was wrong—that her illness had progressed to a new level. One evening as she was preparing for bed, I came into her bedroom and asked her how she was doing. She didn't answer, so I sat down on the edge of her bed and she looked at me with sad eyes.

"What is it, Mom? Is there something I can do for you?"

She only stared back at me, then leaned over to her night-stand and shook out the entire contents of the small prescription bottle. She looked at the handful of pills in her hand and then back up at me.

"What are you saying, Mom? You want to take all these pills? You want to end it?" My heart started beating faster, a mix of fear and anger rising within me.

She only gave a wry smile and shrugged her shoulders, as if to say, *Would that be so bad?*

"No, Mom. That's not how it's going to happen. I'm sorry, but I can't be a party to that." I took the pills out of her hands and put them back into the bottle. She continued to look at me like a child who'd had her lollipop taken away, a mixture of sad resignation and disappointment. I hugged her and said good night and took the bottle with me. I knew this was going to be a short road for my mother. She had lost her will to live, and there was nothing I could do to change that. By the end of the holiday, I had convinced my mother to let me find a caregiver to come a few times a week to help her out at home. She put up a big fight, but in the end she allowed me to do it.

My mother cycled through a few caregivers over the next few months, complaining that they weren't helpful or that they were stealing from her. I never really knew if she was making these things up or not, but I finally found a caregiver who could match my mother's passive resistance to being taken care of. Ironically enough, Sharon, her new caregiver, was about the same age and height as my mother. They were like two peas in a pod, hovering just over five feet tall, small yet fierce. When my mother said she didn't feel like eating, Sharon would kindly ignore her, make a small folded omelet, and leave it in front of my mother wearing her down until she took a few bites. Sharon was practical and resourceful on the outside, but kind and caring on the inside. Her husband was also dying at home, and I couldn't believe she had the emotional capacity to take care of my mother as well. She told me that my mother had become a friend and that this friendship gave her strength to help to take care of her husband. A perfect match found in the most unlikely situation to be sure. The two of them would outwardly snarl at each other, arguing about who was to do what and when, but secretly they leaned on each other and looked forward to their time together.

In March, Nadia and I were back in Las Vegas for my brother's wedding. When I saw my mother, I was appalled by how she looked. She had continued to lose weight since Christmas, and the effects of her stroke a few years earlier had worsened, making her speech more slurred and hardly intelligible. To make matters worse, she had fallen and hit the edge of the coffee table, so she had a bruise and a cut on her forehead. She looked more like my grandmother than my mother, and my heart melted as I saw her. Perhaps it was this shift in my perspective that allowed me to be a little gentler with her and not hold her up to the impossibly high bar that I had my entire life. As we sat on the sofa the day before the wedding, I tried once again to engage her in conversation, and as was our pattern, she turned on the TV—the ever-present familial distraction. I resisted the urge to numb out or get angry with her, as I knew it was time to have a serious discussion with her about her long-term care. It was clear, at least to me, that she was beyond being able to take care of herself, but each time I broached the subject of senior living with her she reacted very negatively. I tried once more.

"Mom, can we please talk about getting you some help? I can see it's very hard for you to take care of yourself, and I'm worried you're going to really hurt yourself and no one will be here."

Silence.

"Mom, I'm really not trying to convince you to move into a nursing home. I'm just trying to understand what you want so I can help you . . ."

She turned her body completely away from me and toward the TV, grabbing the remote to turn the volume up. I felt the familiar frustration rise in me, but this time, instead of raising my voice in anger, I summoned all the patience I could muster and deliberately dropped into compassion as I gently reached out and turned off the TV.

"Mom, can you please talk to me? Please? I'll do whatever you like. I won't force you to move out of your house if that's not what you want, but I need to understand what you'd like to do."

Silence.

A long time passed as we sat in this silence. No background noise coming from the TV, just a soft hum from the refrigerator in the kitchen. I waited. I do not know where I found this patience, but I fell into the peace that was created between us in that moment. Then my mother slowly turned her head back to me and said, "I just don't understand."

I tilted my head as if to say, *Understand what?*

"I...miss...your...dad," she sobbed as she enunciated every word, fighting against her damaged speech, dropping each word like a stone on a path leading to a place we had never been together.

All I could do in that moment was nod my head in understanding. I was shocked by this admission—more by the vulnerability of the statement than the content. There had never been such intimacy between us.

She continued. "I don't understand it. I spent my life fighting with him, wishing he were gone, and now . . . now, I miss him so much." She shifted into remorse. "I was not very nice to him before he died. I was so mad at him for so long, and now I feel so bad. He was my rock, my strength . . . Turns out I don't know how to live without him." She trailed off, as if pondering this personal revelation.

Now I was crying alongside her, nodding in understanding. "Well, he was your husband, despite the battles. I understand how you feel, I really do." I knew all too well that losing someone in the middle of a struggle is even harder than when the relationship is in a good place because of the guilt and the remorse. For my mom, this battle had defined her adult life. In a way, her raison d'être had vanished.

We sat in silence once more.

Then she turned to me. "Wait," she said. "This is what happened to you. You lost your husband too." She looked me in the eyes for the first time. This admission was like a bucket of ice water being thrown on top of my head. After fifty years on this earth, my mother *saw me,* and it had happened when I finally gave up and just allowed myself to be present with her and for her without any expectation. "How do you do it?" she asked me with genuine interest and curiosity for what felt like the first time in my life.

"I do it every day, one day at a time," I replied, basking in the moment I had waited for my entire life. I'm sure she had no idea how much that conversation meant to me. The irony was not lost on me that I finally got what I had always wanted from my mother the minute I let go of my unspoken disappointment in her. I had forgiven her for not being there for me, and she felt it. Once I accepted her and loved her for who she was, she was able to do the same with me. A lifetime of unspoken regrets came to an end. I was finally strong enough to stay with the discomfort of the moment. I resisted numbing out and created a space for both of us to land and was rewarded by having the most intimate moment with my mother I would ever have. She had finally seen me, and I was able to show her how much I loved her without any judgment for the past.

The weekend passed quickly with wedding events, and Nadia and I left Vegas, promising we would be back soon.

As spring gave way to early summer, I noticed that each passing conversation with my mother on the phone got shorter and shorter. It was more difficult for her to enunciate her words and harder for me to understand her. Sharon became my lifeline to my mother as her speech degraded and it became almost impossible for me to understand what she was saying on the phone. Gradually our conversations ended after only a few minutes where I would say, "Okay, Mom, I'll check in with you later this week. I love you." Many times, she wouldn't even say goodbye. She would just hang up the phone, which always felt so jarring to me. One day as I was working through a thorny problem at work, my body began to buzz and my ears began to ring. All of a sudden, my mother popped into my head and a voice said, *You need to go see your mother NOW.* I remembered the same feeling when I talked to the nurse about my father, but this time, I did not allow myself to numb out. I jumped to action.

Within minutes I was on the phone with Sharon, checking in on my mother. Her nonchalance juxtaposed against my heightened anxiety could not stop the growing dread I felt inside me. It did not matter what I was hearing. I knew this feeling. This was the feeling I'd had right before my father died—an oily, queasy, uneasy churning in the pit of my stomach. The feeling I overrode with my mind three years earlier, rationalizing it away. I would not make that mistake again. It was as if I were on autopilot; once I decided that I needed to go see her, I began to make plans to be out of work for a longer period of time. I asked to take family leave for the summer, stating that my mother was ill and that she needed me. This was before there was any indication there was anything truly wrong. I just knew. That weekend I flew to Las Vegas and saw my mother for what turned out to be the last time she was alert and coherent. As I walked into her home, my heart began to race.

It had been two months since I had seen her at my brother's wedding, but I couldn't reconcile the woman in front of me with my mother. The deadness in her eyes haunted me and communicated quite clearly her disinterest in life. She didn't even seem to take pleasure in the ubiquitous cigarette that dangled from her mouth. I had long given up on pleading with her to stop smoking and almost marveled at how she was able to continue inhaling when she barely had the strength to speak or to eat. We were now, both of us, staring down her mortality: my mother with the help of pain medication; me, stone-cold sober, and worse, after losing Daniel and my father, I dared not use my go-to coping mechanism of distraction lest I miss important cues of my mother's eventual demise. So, I did the next best thing: I moved into action.

"Hi, Momma, how are you?" I said in my gentlest voice as I made my way to the sofa where she reclined with a blanket over her. This scene, this feeling of me entering the house from the garage entrance and making my way into the family room to see my mother molded into the sofa, had started feeling familiar. She had become one with the sofa. As I approached, I saw that her eyes were barely open, and it took her a few moments to register I was there. All I could think was, *I made it.* She looked weak, frail and despondent. I was so glad I had finally listened to that voice inside of me and had come. I sat next to her and held her hand. She barely acknowledged my presence. *This is it,* I thought.

"Hi, Mom," I repeated, a little more audibly this time. "Would you like me to get you anything? A cup of tea or a glass of water? Would you like me to make you some soup?" I wanted to do something for her, to ease her suffering even just for a moment. She looked at me through her one good eye, the other practically blind from her glaucoma. "I'm here, Momma. You can go back to sleep if you like." And with that, she laid her head down and fell right back to sleep.

This is how I spent the last weekend with my mother. We did not venture more than a few feet from that sofa, and we didn't need to. It felt good just to be with her. At the end of the weekend, I gave her a big hug and was stunned by how little there was of her to hold. I loosened my grip, afraid I would hurt her, but held on as long as I could. As I pulled out of her driveway in my rental car, I felt a surge of anguish come up through my body and involuntarily erupted into sobs, knowing full well this was the beginning of the end for her.

Two weeks later, Nadia and I had reservations at an annual San Francisco family camp outside Yosemite where at least ten other San Francisco families would be camping alongside us. Nadia loved this annual ritual as it offered her an independence not to be found in the city. She and her posse spent the entire week with their bike helmets on their heads as they jumped on and off their bikes in between cabins, the lake, and their many activities. I was worried about being out of touch as there was no Wi-Fi at camp, so every day I borrowed a friend's bike and rode up the hill to a nearby hotel so I could call Sharon and check on my mother. The second day of camp, Sharon announced that my mom wasn't doing well and that she was going to be transferred to a hospice facility just for a few days to regulate her medication for her pain levels.

"Sharon, should I come home? I can leave right now. Is this it?"

"I don't know, honey," Sharon answered slowly. "Why don't you let me see how it goes, and I can let you know. This is not a long-term facility, so if it looks like she can't come home in a few days, we'll probably need to find a longer-term solution, but she can't take care of herself anymore."

"Okay," was all I could say for a moment, the lump in my throat preventing words from coming out. "I'll have to call you because I have no reception here at camp." I hung up the phone and looked out the window at the pine trees in the distance. *It's happening; it's really happening.* I felt nauseous and my body felt heavy, unable to move for a long time.

I rode back and forth to that hotel two to three times a day over the next couple of days, each time terrified as to what Sharon would tell me. To my surprise, Sharon announced that my mother was doing better. She was alert and had even eaten some food. I was elated, not understanding that this was to be "the last good day," a concept I later learned is quite common before someone passes away. Sure enough, two days later Sharon told me I had better come see her.

I packed up my cabin and all of our belongings and began the long drive back to San Francisco that night, exhausted from a week of camping and the emotional strain of my mother's impending death. Nadia was remarkably chatty the first part of our long ride home. I thought about a time when my mother came to visit us in San Francisco when Nadia was only four years old and we drove through the Presidio, pointing out beautiful sites for my mom to see. Nadia was strapped into her booster seat in the back of the car, adding her own colorful commentary.

"Grandma, this is where we had my birthday party last year." Nadia pointed to a playground tucked under big redwood trees with peek-a-boo views of the Golden Gate Bridge and water just beyond. "I had a jumpy house and a Nemo birthday cake." She was peddling her legs back and forth as she shared more details about her birthday party.

"What else can you remember from that day?" I had prompted. "Did you go to the playground too?

Her eyes lit up. "Yes! A bunch of us went on the big saucer swing, but I wasn't scared," she added confidently. "And then we climbed the big tower made of rope, and it turned into a merry-go-round. That made me dizzy."

On it went like this throughout our scenic drive, when suddenly my mother laughed out loud. When I asked what was funny, she simply said, "You sure do talk a lot to her." I smiled back, not really understanding what she meant, but as I now listened to Nadia chirping away in the back seat and reflected on that moment, I realized that my mother had noticed that I was much more present for my daughter than she ever was for me.

I recalled many stories I had tried to share with my mother when I was young when in mid-sentence, she would walk out the kitchen door into the garage, appearing a minute or two later, saying, "I'm listening, I'm listening, go on, go on . . ." This made me so angry because I knew she wasn't listening to me. I would test her and say, "How could you be listening when you left the room? What did I say then? Tell me. What did I say?" This usually ended with her waving me off with her hand and grabbing a load of laundry to go fold it in another room away from me. As an adult, now I can understand that she was just an overwhelmed mother, but at the time, her inability to take time to listen to me contributed to my resentment of her. Perhaps I was so engaged with Nadia because I was overcompensating for what I didn't get in that way. Perhaps by filling her cup, I was also filling mine.

As we got out of the mountains, I looked into Nadia's eyes through the rearview mirror and calibrated myself to the rhythm of her speech so I could get a word in. "Nadia, sweetie, I think

Grandma Nadia is probably going to die very soon." I held my breath, waiting for her reaction to this news. My poor child, another death before she even turned eight years old. It broke my heart to have to tell her. She had seen as much death as I had in forty years.

I saw her look down at Brittany, her polar bear stuffie, and begin to reply. "I know, Mom. She didn't look good at Uncle Jason's wedding." She raised her head and looked out the window and said, "I love Grandma Nadia." And then to my utter surprise, she looked back into my eyes through the mirror and asked, "Are you okay, Momma?"

Wow. Wow. What an amazing child. My heart was stuck in my throat as it so often was when I was around Nadia in times of emotional intensity. Her level of caring and empathy was always such a surprise. "Yes, sweetie, I'm okay. I'm sad, but Grandma has been sick for a long time and it's good she won't suffer too much longer."

She simply nodded her head and started to play with Brittany. I saw she was getting tired, and soon she was fast asleep, propped up by camping equipment, pillows, and blankets. I drove the rest of the way home thinking about the magically emotionally resilient little creature in my back seat and hoping and praying she would continue to blossom in the way that she was. *Stay open, Momma,* I thought. *Give her the space to feel, be present with her, and mostly just show her that you see her and love her just as she is.*

The next morning, I unpacked, washed, and repacked a bag to board my flight for Las Vegas later that day. I phoned Michael to explain to him that my mother was dying and asked him if he thought it was okay for Nadia to come to Las Vegas. "Absolutely," he replied. "She is prepared to experience the normal death of her grandmother. I'm sorry for your loss, too, Laila. Let me know how it goes."

Not knowing what I would be facing or how long it would take for my mother to pass away, I decided to leave Nadia at home with Marci and have Marci fly out after me when the timing became clearer.

Meanwhile, I had been trying to reach my brother and sister to make sure they would make it to my mother's bedside as well. They both lived in Las Vegas and, like me, had inherited the family trait of denial, but I was compelled to do the right thing for once in my life and get them to my mother's bedside. My younger sister and her daughter had been estranged from the family for close to ten years after a falling-out with my mother. I never really knew the details, nor did I want to know, quite frankly. But now, it was if a shroud had been lifted from my eyes, and for the first time, I had clarity; I allowed myself to feel the impending loss of my mother. I had deluded myself that Daniel was all right, I had ignored the little voice inside that said, *Go see your dad now*. I'd be damned if I was going to allow myself to sleep through a third loss in as many years. *No more,* I told myself resolutely. *It's time to get real and to feel it all.*

Getting through to my brother and sister proved to be more difficult than I thought.

It took me a few days to get a good phone number for my sister. It had been years since we had spoken, and I remembered how difficult it could be for us to see eye to eye on just about anything. I finally got her on the line.

"Maya, Mom is dying," I said. "I wanted to make sure I let you know so you can go see her before she passes away." I tried to imagine what it was like for my sister to hear these words after not having seen my mother for so long. I tried to be gentle yet convey the urgency.

"Well, you know, I'm not sure I can do that," she said.

"What do you mean?" I didn't understand if this was more of an emotional or a logistical constraint, so I started offering solutions, as was my way. "Do you need a ride?"

"No, I mean, she hasn't been very nice to us . . ." And then she launched into a soliloquy of the problems and arguments that had transpired between them, making an argument for her absence and disconnection from the family.

I tuned out completely. It felt like I was on another planet. *What the hell was she talking about, and what did it matter at a time like this?* Then the strangest thing happened. I caught myself moving from anger to numbness, not wanting to deal with the situation, but then I made the conscious decision to stay present. I breathed through my anger, pushed through my numbness, and thought solely of my mother and about what I needed to do to get her daughter by her side.

"Maya, I understand what you're saying, I really do, but do you understand what I'm telling you right now? She is dying. Your mother—the only one you will ever have—will not be here much longer. I'm quite sure that you will regret this if you do not see her before she goes. Please, can you just try to go see her? Please."

There was a long silence on the phone. I resisted the urge to ask again, to plead, to erupt in judgment and contempt. Finally, I heard her take a breath and sigh.

"I don't know if I can. I will let you know."

As much as I wanted to dismiss her objections, I couldn't. I knew what she meant. She wasn't sure if she could emotionally handle seeing my mother on her deathbed after shunning her for a decade. Had I not been doing so much work to access my heart, I could have easily been my sister. Our mother wasn't perfect, to be sure, and I had wrestled my whole life with accepting her for who she was. I was certain my incessant drive to action was directly related to my mother's inaction. I had to act for the both of us and had spent a lifetime resenting her because she wasn't strong and capable. So, I became strong and capable instead. But why? Why had I chosen this path while my sister had chosen another? I considered many explanations, justifications, and rationalizations, but ultimately it came down to two things. First, I never gave up hope that one day, my mother and I would connect on a deeper level. The second factor was having the ability to self-reflect and work on seeing the role I played in our relationship and dedicating myself to a path of self-awareness and discovery. Those two things led me back to my mother and ultimately myself, which was a journey it seemed that my sister was still unable to take. I felt bad for her, for her suffering, and for the time she lost with our mother, but I knew in that moment I couldn't say anything else to move her off her position. I thanked her for her time and said goodbye.

Over the next twenty-four hours, I channeled as much love, compassion, and patience as I could muster into an ongoing text conversation with my sister to try to convince her to go see our mom. This was not easy for me, as I often found her to be irrational and unforgiving. Finally, I offered the biggest olive branch I could. "Maya," I texted, "I will come to your house if you like, and I will be with you the entire time. I know this is hard, but I think it's really important for her and for you, and I will be by your side the whole time, okay? Please?"

"Okay," she relented. "You don't have to come get me. Just send me the address."

"I will. Thank you. Please hurry. I will be there, so just let me know when you're coming."

When I arrived in Las Vegas, it felt odd not to drive to my mother's home. I took a left turn instead of a right when I got to my mother's side of town and made my way to the hospice facility. When I walked into my mother's room, I saw her curled up on her side, just a whisper of a person. Her skin was sallow, and her face was gaunt. Her eyes were closed. There were several people in the room: Sharon, my aunt and uncle, and a few cousins I had not seen in some time. I met their eyes but went straight to my mother.

"Hi, Momma. It's Laila. I'm here," I said, stroking her thin hair, which was half-white and half-brown at this point. I made a mental note that I had to have her hair colored because she would be mortified to go into the afterlife with these roots. As soon as she heard my voice, her eyes fluttered, and she tried to open them. While I'm not sure she actually saw me, I know she knew I had arrived.

Sharon cried out. "Look at how much she's reacting to your voice, Laila! She hasn't moved that much in hours." Her mouth looked dry, so I took a utensil that looked like a toothbrush with a sponge on the end of it, and I dipped it into water and ran it through her mouth. It took everything I had not to break down into a puddle of tears, but I kept my wits about me and eventually left her bedside to greet everyone else.

I then went and took out my computer from my backpack. I went to my iTunes and searched for Deva Premal, my favorite new age spiritual singer, and selected the Gayatri Mantra chant. I put this nine-minute chant on an infinite loop, and it played over and over for the next couple of hours. There were moments when someone would ask, "What was that music?" I would only smile and offer no explanations. This was for my mother and me and no one else. I knew she could hear it, and I hoped it was bringing her comfort in her transition.

I had discovered both the Gayatri Mantra and Deva Premal when I began my yoga practice. We would say the chant before each yoga class, and when I heard Deva Premal's rendition of it, I thought it was one of the most beautiful chants I had ever heard. I memorized the words so I could say the prayer myself. It was one of the oldest and most revered prayers from the Vedic verses, the precursor to Hinduism. I had read that it is a universal prayer that is often played during the passage from one life to the next because the mantra purifies the mind and confers devotion, detachment, and wisdom, making it easier for a person to let go at their moment of death. It also inspires the person to think of others with loving-kindness and compassion, to wish others to be happy and free from suffering. The reasoning was that if a person dies with the thought of benefiting others, their mind is naturally happy, and this makes their death meaningful.

The music had already hooked me, and when I read this description, I knew that I had to play it for my mother. I hoped my mom would hear this music and feel my strength, knowing she had a hand in instilling that strength in me despite rarely being able to stand up for herself. I wondered if courage skipped a generation, or did it just show up in different ways? Who was I to say that my mother was not brave and strong in her own way? She moved across countries and across cultures to give her children a better life with more opportunity. Could there be a braver, more selfless act?

My phone buzzed, and I saw a text from my sister. She had arrived and was in the parking lot. I told her that I was inside in room 311 and asked if she wanted me to come out, but she said no, that she and her daughter, Melissa, would be okay coming in. A few minutes later, I saw both of them standing at the door of my mother's room. The shock of what they saw was fully evident in their reactions. I was shocked by how they looked as well.

My sister, who had always been slim, was now about forty pounds overweight. Melissa, now in her early twenties, had grown to be almost six feet tall. They both wore glasses, so it was difficult to see their eyes, but soon both their faces contorted into looks of anguish as they leaned on each other and then against the doorframe, overcome with emotion. I knew the reality of who my mother had become would be seared in their minds forever. I could not imagine the jolt they must have felt not having seen her decline as I had. For a few minutes, they did not enter, could not enter, but simply stood there as if there was a force field preventing them from coming in.

I spoke to my mother while looking up at my sister. "Mom, Maya's here. She's here to see you . . ." I motioned for my sister to come take my place on the bed near my mother. She slowly approached, wracked with sobs, unable to speak, but took my mother's hand. My mother began to stir again. *Thank you, God,* I thought. She'd made it, and my mom knew that Maya had come to her bedside. I felt a small victory in helping to tie all the pieces together at the end for my mother. I looked over to Melissa, who was still leaning against the door, and motioned her in, but she silently declined, unable to compose herself, yet unable to break her gaze from her mother and grandmother just a few feet away.

As the light dimmed and the hours began to fade into the late afternoon, people started to say their goodbyes, one by one. My sister and Melissa slipped out of the room with hardly a word to anyone. Soon, it was just my mother and me. The room was quiet. I sat with her for a long time just stroking her hand. I phoned my brother, who had not come to see our mother yet.

"Jason, you need to come soon. I don't think she has much time left."

"I have to work tonight and won't get off until two or three in the morning."

"It doesn't matter," I said. "You should just come so she can know that you are here."

I was fully aware that my tendency to duck and hide from all the bad feelings in my life was a deeply inherited family trait. My brother showed the most obvious emotional detachment with his soft, monotone voice hovering somewhere between apathy and annoyance.

"Okay, I'll come," my brother finally replied.

I settled into the daybed that sat against the window just a few feet from my mother's bed and soon fell asleep with an audiobook in my ears. Normally a very light sleeper, I did not hear my brother come see my mother in the middle of the night, nor did he try to wake me. I only barely heard the nurses come in at four in the morning to check on my mother. At six thirty, I awoke with the natural light beginning to come into the room. I was disoriented only a moment before an emotional cocktail of sorrow, trepidation, and unease flooded my body. I got up, brushed my teeth, splashed some water on my face, and set up the Gayatri Mantra on my computer next to my mother's bed. Doing the thing my mother would always do in times of discomfort, I turned on the TV, but I put it on silent. I pulled over a chair and sat next to my mother. Her breathing was extremely labored, and it hurt me to hear how much she was struggling to stay alive. Words began to spill out of my mouth without any premeditation at all.

"Mom," I spoke out loud. "That's enough now. You need to go. Don't worry about anything here. I will take care of everything and everyone. You were a good momma, and I love you very much. Go now. If you see the light, go to it."

I turned my head back to the TV in that moment and read on the scroll bar that Nelson Mandela was also struggling in the hospital and thought what an incredible travel companion he would be for her if they died on the same day. Then I noticed that the markets were down.

"Mom, it looks like Nelson Mandela might be joining you on your journey and the markets are down; they are clearly sad for you." I let out a small laugh at this weak joke, but then I noticed that her breathing had changed, or more precisely, I no longer heard the grunting and wheezing associated with each irregular breath. I turned my face back to my mother and waited.

A few seconds passed.

No noise. No breath.

What? I didn't mean you could go right this second! I touched her arm. It was soft and warm.

"Mom?"

No answer.

I touched her chest to see if there was any movement. No movement.

I started to hyperventilate. I didn't know what to do. I ran out of the room, trying to find the nurses from the day before. One of the male nurses I did not recognize gently pulled me aside and asked, "What's wrong, honey, can I help you?"

"My . . . my...mom . . ." It was impossible to talk because I couldn't breathe.

"Okay, it's okay, can you tell me which room she's in?"

I could only look into his eyes, but no words would come from my mouth. Finally, I held up my fingers. 3 – 1 – 1.

"Okay, room 311, come with me." He put his hand on my back, and I walked with him into my mother's room.

He took a stethoscope out and checked her chest. "I'm sorry, she's gone."

But of course, I already knew this. I nodded my head, tears streaming down my face.

"Would you like me to call the chaplain?"

I nodded my head again.

"Do you know where she's to be buried? You can probably call them and let them know to come get her."

"Okay."

He left the room and I was alone with my mother. The chaplain came and said a prayer for her. I thanked him as he left the room. I turned my attention back to my mother, knowing I needed to start making phone calls but wanting to spend one last moment with her alone. I sat next to her and touched her again and was stunned that she already felt cool to the touch. I grabbed a blanket and put it over her, knowing full well I was being ridiculous, but I didn't care.

"Bye bye, Momma. We love you," was all I could say. I began to make the calls that I knew would move me into administration mode. I phoned the mortuary and started texting family members to let them know she had passed. As I waited for someone to come get her, I replayed the final moments of my mom's life in my head. I was, finally, *finally* supremely aware of how perfect that moment was and what a gift it was for me to be able to usher the person who brought me into this world out of this world with love and compassion. We saw each other and had the ultimate connection we were both searching for our whole lives. The circle was complete for my mother and me. I said a silent prayer to myself. *Thank you, God, for getting me here—physically, emotionally, and spiritually.*

The next ten days were a whirlwind. The truth of the matter was that this was not my first rodeo, and I knew exactly what to do and how to do it. In less than two weeks I wrapped up an entire life, starting with my mother's memorial service. The Greek Orthodox priest who knew my mother was out of town, so I had to meet with another priest and tell him a little about my mom so that he could say a few words at her funeral. Though we had never discussed it, I knew my mother would have wanted this. Entering this big, beautiful church flooded me with memories of my Catholic school upbringing, an odd mixture of leaning into the nostalgia yet pulling away from the dogma. I tried to synthesize the essence of my mother to this priest in our brief meeting.

"My mother was very religious. She was a really good person, very kind to everyone. She always had an altar at home with pictures that looked exactly like the ones you have here leaning against the wall." I realized in that moment that the traditional style of the paintings where everyone had a halo around their head was emblematic of the Greek Orthodox Church. As our conversation broadened out to religion in general, I was pleased that we seemed to generally agree on our concept of God. I started to relax until I heard him move into the "and God will smite you with all his might" part. *Ugh,* I thought. *I don't think I can do this.* I respectfully told him that this is where my views diverged from his and from the Church's, I supposed.

"I believe that God, which is just another way to say the divine, or love or light, is in you. It's not someone or something external to you judging you or punishing you. I doubt we will agree on this point, but if you could please just stay away from the mean, fire-and-brimstone God in your sermon, I would really appreciate it."

He looked at me, smiled, and nodded his head.

I went back to my mother's home and allowed myself to sob for just a few moments before I opened my computer and made my to-do list and started checking items off my list: *Write eulogy, create a DVD, pick out outfit for Mom, have her hair colored, pack up house, list house, sell house.* I paused. *Perhaps I should create sub-bullets for these last three*, I thought.

I poured a glass of water and began the impossible task of packing up a life. Things fell into my lap effortlessly. I know she was helping me. There were loose photos everywhere—piled up in corners in desks, stuffed into boxes and crates in the back of closets, most of them bent, ripped, and/or faded from decades of exposure. There were almost as many sizes of photos as there where photos themselves. I began to organize and group them by size. This inadvertently had the effect of organizing them by time period, as the standard size for photos changed from country to country and decade to decade. Then I went through each pile and separated duplicates before creating a pile for my sister and a pile for my brother, populating those with the duplicates and photos of themselves or their kids. It was overwhelming at times. I was alone in my mom and dad's house and they were gone, and all that was left of them were these memories captured in photos strewn all over the house. It took a long time to go through them, as many of the photos triggered memories that caused me to linger or look for others around that time period, trying to piece together the jigsaw puzzle of our lives.

Then I saw it. The picture of me at nine years old with my pink V-neck sweater tucked into my short pleated plaid skirt and my long, skinny brown legs extending below. I was smiling sweetly into the camera standing in front of our Las Vegas suburban home on Birthday Street. You could see all the seventies muscle cars parked along the curb behind me. I didn't know why, but something about that photo stopped me in my tracks. I felt I needed to be gentle with this one, this one little photo that stood out in the sea of thousands. It made me sad to look into this girl's face and I wanted to protect her, to make space for her to feel and to be happy. I gently tucked her into a book and took her home with me.

Nadia flew out to meet me in Las Vegas and attended my mother's funeral. I wrote what I hoped would be the last eulogy I would need to write and found that the words came easily. Nadia was able to be fully present at my mother's funeral and hardly seemed sad. She had even made some drawings for her and personally put them in the open casket, inspecting my mother's body closely as she reached across her to position her artwork.

"Still looks like Grandma," she whispered, as she touched her face delicately. The reaction to such intimacy on the faces of my family members underscored for me just how far I had come in my ability to stay present with uncomfortable emotions and was further validation that I was doing for my nine-year-old what the nine-year-old in my photo needed too.

CHAPTER 13

FINDING STRENGTH IN SOFTNESS

"We are not meant to be perfect; we are meant to be whole."
—JANE FONDA

Returning back to San Francisco and back to work after burying my mom felt odd. Peet's had just announced that we would be purchased by a private equity firm in Europe, and our new owners had big plans for us. Many of the executives that had been at Peet's were leaving, and I knew it was time for me to move on as well. I had long been thinking about taking a break and moving abroad to give Nadia a chance to improve her French. I began to finalize my plans to resign from Peet's and move to the South of France. Letting Pat know I would be leaving was bittersweet for me. Peet's would always be an important part of my life, but it was time to start a new chapter.

It had been a life-altering journey where my personal and professional lives had come together for the first time to teach me some very valuable lessons. While I would not have chosen to lose my husband, father, and mother in quick succession, it was clear that they provided the necessary catalyst for me to unlock decades of buried and unfelt emotions so that I could heal and grow as a mother and as a leader. A subtle alchemy had come together to complete my personal transformation. I had been tested time and time again, each time learning it was my willingness to lean into the pain and allow myself to be vulnerable that had emerged as my true strength and the true source of my power at home and at work. Strengthening my heart to give it equal playing time alongside my head and connecting the two had been the key to unlocking my personal and professional growth.

As a farewell to Peet's, Pat invited his direct reports out for a goodbye dinner. As dinner was winding down, he turned to all of us and said that he wanted to take a moment to thank each one of us for all we had done for the company. One by one he went around the table relaying a funny story or personal anecdote that high-lighted what he appreciated most about each and every member of the leadership team. As Pat was never one to lavish praise easily, we all held our breath trying to remember every word meant for each of us. When he turned to me, he paused for a moment and looked into my eyes.

"Laila . . ." he pondered, "you were like the yin to all of our yang. There were moments when it felt that we would have certainly leaned too far in one direction had you not provided the counterbalance. I know that couldn't have been easy for you, and I appreciate the courage it took to put yourself out there, always trying to do the right thing for the people and the company."

I was in shock. It was as if he could see right through me. Shawn leaned over and whispered to me, "He sure got that right . . ." I smiled back at him, barely able to hold back my tears. I knew that my journey to connect my head to my heart was what I needed to grow in my personal life, but I never truly realized how much it was seen and valued professionally. I had spent sixteen months rolling out the company values under the banner of "Bring Your Whole Self to Work," but of course, there were two sides to this equation: the company side, in which I tried to create the conditions for everyone to feel safe enough to show all of themselves, *and* the personal side where each person needed to do their own work to become whole, including me. I was reminded of an Oprah Master Class video I had seen recently where Jane Fonda shared, "Many decades it took me to learn to not be afraid of saying how I feel, and to allow my vulnerabilities to show—we are not meant to be perfect; we're meant to be whole." The yin and the yang, the head and the heart, the masculine and the feminine, strong and soft, together, combined. Turns out it's never either/or; it's always both.

I made an appointment to see Dr. Michael Litter one last time to get advice from him about our impending move to France.

"You're ready, Laila, and so is Nadia. It's a perfect time in Nadia's life for you to take a year off of work and have this grand adventure together. Luckily for us, Nadia has been a very effective user of therapy. Working with her has been like taking a baseball bat to a fire hydrant. She came in here week after week and started playing and working through her emotions. There are kids I see around Nadia's age or a year or two older and it's difficult to get a word out of them all session."

In that moment, I felt proud in being able to provide a safe space for Nadia to process her feelings, and I was grateful that she had become my teacher to do the samee. *Better late than never.*

"As I've said before, Nadia is a genius in how she uses imaginary play. She continues to amaze me in how she's able to process very deep feelings through her play. She spins the richest world full of her emotions and what she's struggling with. It is critical she takes the time to sort through how she's feeling."

"Critical for me too, I think . . ." I mumbled as I finished typing my notes of the session.

"Critical for all of us," he repeated.

Here was the same lesson coming up again. *We all need space to know how we feel.*

It was time to let go of Daniel's ashes. While it hadn't been my intention, I had been holding on to them for almost five years after missing my opportunity to spread his ashes the day of his memorial due to the huge storm that had hit San Francisco that day. Instead I brought them back home and hoisted the square wooden urn up onto a bookshelf in our living room, looking down at our then three-year-old daughter's face. Perhaps this was for the best, I had thought, perhaps the right time would be when Nadia would be old enough to remember saying goodbye to her father. So the ashes had remained in that wooden urn with a carving of the Golden Gate Bridge etched into the front panel. The urn had looked down on us as we tried to make sense of our loss. At first, it was oddly comforting to have him back in the house. From time to time, Nadia and I would speak out loud to him about the day's events. After the first anniversary of his death, I moved him to a shelf above the closet in the guest bedroom, feeling we needed more distance. Eventually, I had asked his sister Stephanie to hold on to him until we were ready to let go. With our impending move to the South of France, I knew we needed to spread his ashes as closure before we moved.

We chose August 9, the five-year anniversary of Daniel's birthday, to release his ashes into the sea. The weather in August on the Northern California coast could be more like Scotland than San Diego. The morning was, as expected, cool and foggy, but a gentle breeze was already pushing the fog offshore, and I was hopeful the sun would break through soon to warm the day. We walked single file on a narrow, winding dirt path leading to Muir Beach. As we approached the shore, we caught glimpses of the Pacific Ocean in the distance, dark and gray under the clouds. I stared down at the square urn and remembered how easy it had been for me to choose this container for Daniel; it captured his love of the water perfectly. The song "Daniel" by Elton John played off my tiny cell phone speakers accompanying us to the shore. Jared, a dear friend and Zen Buddhist priest, was dressed in formal robes. He led the way as Nadia, now nine years old, walked between us. In her hand she held three red balloons, which bobbed up and down as she walked, keeping time with the bobbing of her high blonde ponytail. In her other hand, she clutched three yellow long-stemmed roses with Brittany, her little polar bear stuffie, wedged securely under her armpit. To know Nadia was to know Brittany, the teeny-tiny face of that small white polar bear peeking out from under her arm in every picture taken from three years old on.

Arriving at the beach, we nestled into a natural cutout in the cliffs. Jared smoothed out the sand and placed rocks in a wide circle to enclose the space. We set our things down on the damp sand, and Jared kicked off the ceremony with a prayer. As he finished his prayer, I stood up and replaced him in the center of the circle. I slowly began to unfold the copy of the eulogy I had read five years earlier at Daniel's memorial.

I glanced at Nadia, her eyes shiny and present, waiting for me to begin. How had five years vanished so quickly? I flashed on her face five years earlier—her beautiful baby face, fuller, with wispy, thin blonde curls falling around her neck, sitting on my lap in the velvet dress we had bought for Christmas. And me—tired, thin, trying to make sense of the tragedy that had befallen us, leaving me a widow at forty-three years old. She had no real understanding of what was happening around her on that day, but as I looked in her eyes this morning, five and a half years later, her face narrower, her long, thick hair a shade darker, I knew today's reading would land in a much more conscious place for both of us.

"Thank you for coming today . . ." I began the same eulogy I had recited almost five years earlier, glancing up intermittently to check on Nadia and to take in everything around me— the rocks jutting out of the sand, the sea in the distance, the breeze begin-ning to warm as the sun rose in the sky. Unlike the first reading, I wanted to take it all in today. Five years of active healing had loosened the constriction around my heart and my airways so that I could breathe more easily than at the first reading, when my heart was crushed under the weight of his recent loss.

"Marriage changed Daniel, but nothing like fatherhood. For a man who appreciated the finer things in life, he understood immediately that the most important thing—that the finest thing of all—was his love for his daughter." I looked up and saw Nadia had tuned in more closely when she entered the story. I gave her a wry smile and continued to read. When I finished, Nadia stood up and replaced me in the center of the circle, reading, "How Do I Love Thee" by Elizabeth Barrett Browning.

"What do you think you'd like to say?" I had asked her as we were having breakfast at the kitchen counter one day.

She shrugged, looking down at the hardwood floor. "I don't know, I guess that I still love him."

Of course, she wanted to tell her daddy that she still loved him. I remembered a drawing she had done at school with three stick figures shortly after Daniel's death—Nadia and me on the ground, holding hands, and Daniel floating above us in the air with wings, our angel up in heaven smiling down on us. "It's our family portrait," she proclaimed. I could only nod and smile to see how she was keeping him alive.

"How about this one?" I pulled my computer screen over so she could read "How Do I Love Thee."

"Yes, that's it," she agreed.

The wind picked up and gently blew long strands of thin blonde hair across Nadia's face as she finished her piece. "I love thee with the breath, smiles, tears of all my life; and, if God choose, I shall but love thee better after death."

She looked down at her sheet of paper, and I tugged her close to wipe a single tear from her cheek as she nuzzled her face into my fleece jacket. It had been a summer filled with loss for us. Shortly after my mother's death only a month and a half earlier, inconceivably, Kevin, a dear classmate of Nadia's had lost his long battle with brain cancer just a few days before. Feeling the need to help, I had been given the task of putting the final touches on the announcement to the school community and had attended his wake at St. Gabriel Church only the night before. We were, both of us, emotionally spent, the sadness for each loss intermingling inside us, leaving us heavy and numb.

The only thing keeping me from recoiling into a deep, dark hole was the knowledge that we would soon be spending a blissful year in the South of France. One year of freedom—no work, all play. I had started planning this move long before my mother's health had turned, before Kevin's cancer came out of remission, and before I had decided we would be spreading Daniel's ashes. In a way, it felt like I had been living parallel and separate lives: one focused on honoring each and every loss over the summer, and the other planning for our new life ahead. On the surface, the administrative details of closing out a life and moving to a foreign country were strangely similar, but the emotional energy associated with each of them was vastly different. One was closing, and one was opening; one was focused on the past—memories and regrets—the other focusing on the future, full of hope and possibilities. The emotional polarity of these two concurrent realities blended to make me appear "normal." To the casual observer, I appeared to be emotionally grounded and balanced. Inside, there were times I felt like I was holding on to a vicious emotional roller coaster, white-knuckled and nauseated, praying for the ride to end.

Just at that moment, the sun broke through the last of the fog and the sea transformed from dark gray to deep blue. I removed the top of the urn, revealing a plastic bag with white-gray ashes settled inside. I paused for a moment. *This* was Daniel? *This* is what we are all reduced to in the end? *Ashes to ashes, dust to dust* . . . Like an image coming into sharp focus through a photo lens, I experienced a moment of deep connection with all who came before me and those after me as if we were all on some kind of cosmic continuum of beings, until I lost sense of where I started and where they began. Just for an instant—a millisecond, really—I was able to experience myself beyond my physical body and feel into my infinite expansiveness as part of all that ever was and will be.

I leaned down and offered the open container to Nadia. "Shall we set him free?" She smiled at me and scooped out two fistfuls of ashes without hesitation. She ran toward the shoreline flinging the ashes into the breaking waves.

"Bye, Daddy!" Nadia yelled. "Happy birthday, Daddy. We love you!" She ran back for more ashes to release.

"Goodbye, Grandma," I added, throwing one of the yellow roses into the sea.

Nadia smiled and grabbed the other yellow rose, yelling, "Goodbye, Kevin, we will miss you! Daddy and Grandma, please take care of Kevin up in heaven and help him not be scared." My beautiful child. She was always saying things that stopped me in my tracks, and why would today be any different?

"Mom, can we please keep some of Daddy with us?" Nadia asked as we got to the end of the ashes. It was unsettling to hear her refer to his ashes directly as "Daddy."

I nodded, unable to say anything as my throat was choked up. These ashes were indeed him—at least what was left of the physical manifestation of him on this earth. Kids are so concrete in their thinking.

Jared found a small shell in the sand and picked out three tiny pebbles, placing them delicately into the shell to symbolize our family, and handed it to Nadia. She placed the shell with the remaining ashes into the now largely empty urn and declared that she was sure Daddy would like to live there. Jared and I could only exchange glances with each other and nod in agreement.

We gathered our things and began to head back to the path.

"Nadia, do you want to let the balloons go so they can fly up to heaven to be with Daddy?" I suggested gently.

Nadia frowned at me, then reluctantly agreed, never one to let go of a balloon for any reason. The three red balloons slowly rounded the mountain and danced along the edge, refusing to fly away. We followed them along the path back to the parking lot and watched them in silence as they ascended high into the sky.

"They're with Daddy now," Nadia stated definitively.

We hugged Jared goodbye and went to have brunch at the Dipsea Café. We sat side by side at the table eating mostly in silence, then drove home, put our nighties back on, and crawled back into bed. Nadia curled into a little ball next to me, and I stroked her hair until she fell asleep. It wasn't even noon.

Ten days later we boarded a flight for Nice—making space to feel.

Epilogue

"Owning our story and loving ourselves through that process is the bravest thing that we will ever do."

—Brené Brown

I curled into a patio chair overlooking medieval chateaux perched atop beautiful green hills with and olive trees sprinkled upon them. The Mediterranean sun warmed my face as I gazed upon my pool and took in the beauty around me. A mixture of jasmine and citrus scents wafted throughout the garden, and the intermittent buzz of a bee brought me back out of my half-dream state. I had done it. It had been six weeks since Nadia and I moved to the South of France, and I was enjoying my cappuccino in my gorgeous backyard, taking in my new life. Glancing at my watch, I realized it was time to pick Nadia up from school.

I wound my way through the hilly roads, capturing a glimpse of the Med on my right and the French Alps on my left. I parked my car in a small parking lot surrounded by woods and made my way up to a small building with a large blue sign on it that said "EBICA, Ecole Bilingue Internationale Côte d'Azur." Standing in the narrow hallways of Nadia's new school, I searched the jostling sea of small people seeking their parental match. My eyes caught Nadia's gaze across the corridor, and she ran to me, falling forward with the weight of her backpack.

"Mommy!" She wrapped her thin arms around me.

"Hi, Bug! How was your day?" I gazed down at her, pulling loose strands of her blonde pigtails back from her flushed cheeks.

"Awesome," came her standard answer.

"What was awesome about it?"

"Well, the French teacher is so nice, Mommy, and I met a British girl named Natalia who I really like, and I want you to meet her because I want to go to her house and play . . ."

Just then, another little girl with light strawberry blonde hair bounded up and exclaimed in a very proper British accent, "Hello, I'm Natalia. Please come meet my mum so Nadia can come to my house."

Nadia pulled me by the hand through the sea of kids to a beautiful blonde woman, her hair pulled back into a low ponytail, wearing a sundress and light makeup that framed her face perfectly. She had the most exotic accent as she said, "Oh, hello. Yes, I'm Agnieszka, Natalia's mum. You're very welcome to follow me home so the girls can play, and we can get to know each other."

"Yes, that would be wonderful," I replied. Driving to Agnieszka's home, I said a little thank-you to the universe for giving me this time with my daughter. So this was what it felt like to pick your child up at school rather than work all day and come home three hours later, homework finished, dinner eaten, and teeth brushed. My heart hurt a little as I saw what I had been missing. In the back of my car, Nadia and Natalia were chatting away, ignorant of my prying ears up front, and I dared not say a word as I got a rare glimpse into my daughter's emerging social skills.

Turning into Agnieszka's driveway, we waited for oversized automatic iron gates to open, granting us entry into a grand old two-story French villa. Nadia held my hand as we entered the foyer, looking up at me, clearly excited about her new playmate. As it was very hot out, the girls immediately ran to Natalia's room to change into bathing suits.

"Would you like a glass of rosé?" Agnieszka asked.

"Yes, that would be lovely," I responded as I settled into a rattan sectional with oversized cushions overlooking the girls playing in the pool and the rolling hills just beyond. Bringing the rosé to my lips, I couldn't help but feel wobbly as I thought about what I would have been doing just a few weeks earlier at this time of day. There were so many versions of life to live, and how quickly things can change.

Swimming and rosé gave way to dinner outside, and as the sun set we said our goodbyes, driving the short distance back to our home. After tucking Nadia into her bed that evening, I kissed her and walked across the living room to my bedroom. Within minutes, Nadia appeared at my bedroom door with Brittany tucked under her arm. She pulled the now-tattered, off-white little bear from under her arm and swung Brittany's body back and forth in front of my face.

"Brittany wants to say good night to you."

This had become our ritual since arriving in France. "Brittany" wanted to say good night.

"Shall we do a group hug?" I asked. Nadia nodded before flinging herself onto me and plopping into my bed, looking up at me with her big brown eyes.

"Nadia, would you like to sleep with me—" Before I could complete my sentence, she pulled the covers up to her neck and nuzzled herself and Brittany against my side. I tried to extricate my one free arm to grab the new book I had recently purchased on the best of the Côte d'Azur so that I could read as she pressed herself against me.

"I love you, Mommy," she whispered as a thank-you, I think, for her new life.

"I love you too, Buggie." My heart swelled with love and gratitude for our new life, for the love of this beautiful angel of mine, and for the gift of time with her. Soon enough, she was breathing heavily next to me and my eyes felt heavy from the wine. I searched for a bookmark to save my place in my book and saw the tiny picture of my nine-year-old self fall out of the pages. I stared at this photo a long time before using it as a bookmark and laying my book down on my nightstand.

Snuggling against Nadia, I realized that I no longer had to take on the weight of the world as that nine-year-old girl felt she needed to. I didn't have to save everyone to be loved. My mind flashed on the many heroic roles I was convinced I needed to play my entire life, starting with my very first one trying to break up my parents' fight, making myself my mother's protector, unnaturally reversing our roles wherein I became the responsible mother and she, the needy child. By the time I met Daniel, despite my efforts to heal my emotional wounds, I was unable to resist the pull to try to fix him, to rescue him—to try to be his hero. From Daniel, I learned the greatest lesson of all—trying to be the hero for someone who cannot be rescued comes from a broken and unhealed place. Failing to rescue Daniel was the ultimate lesson in teaching me to let go of the hero persona that had kept me emotionally isolated my whole life.

I felt my body relax as I allowed sleep to fall over me, but not before one clear thought crystalized in my brain before settling deeply into my heart.

These days, I can't even be Nadia's hero. I can't rescue her from life's tragedies. I can only support her with an open heart. The only person for whom I can be ultimately responsible is the nine-year-old girl inside of me.

While physically, my journey had taken me to France, my inner journey brought me back to the little girl in that picture. I fought mightily along the way, fearful that my journey would make me soft—and it did, but soft turned out to be strong. It seemed appropriate that in the end, I wound up being the hero—no, not the hero—*the heroine* of my own story.

Acknowledgments

This book would never have seen the light of day without the support and encouragement of a vast group of people. I would like to thank the following people who were instrumental in my journey as a writer:

She Writes Press, Brooke Warner, and the entire SWP team for their guidance throughout the publishing process. Your professionalism made me feel like I was in the hands of experts.

Jennie Nash, who provided me with the structure, support, and encouragement I needed to untangle my thoughts and get them down on the page. Thank you for believing in me and this book.

Laura Munson, through her Haven Writing Retreat in the summer of 2015, gave me my first taste of writing and made me believe I could write. Thank you for creating such a beautiful community of writers.

Anna Geller, who was instrumental in connecting me with my publisher and was a wise and patient mentor in educating me on the business of publishing every step of the way.

Dan Roam, for encouraging me from the very beginning and showing me the way. You were able to envision this book long before I could imagine it myself. Your conviction and continued support were instrumental in my never giving up.

Carter Cast, for his quiet encouragement along the way, and Paul Coletta, for his ongoing support and inspiration for the title.

Lisa Ames, Lisa Campagna, Heather Corcoran, and Debbie Kristofferson—my close friends who endured years of me working through an idea on our beautiful hikes in Marin.

My teachers, mentors, and support structure I have been fortunate to assemble along the way: In business: Jeanne Jackson, Carter Cast, and Pat O'Dea. My New Ventures West coaching community: James Flaherty, Marina Illich, and especially Kathrin O'Sullivan. My wise therapists: Dr. Robert Okin and Dr. Michael Ritter. And my constant cheerleaders: Marci Nelson, Amy Lester, and Jodi Bricker.

Finally, to my beautiful and precious Nadia, who looks up to me as if I could do no wrong. You are the inspiration for all I do. I know that I can never give up so that I can show you that life is not the destination but the journey.

ABOUT THE AUTHOR

L aila Tarraf is a senior human resource executive with over twenty-five years of professional experience. After graduating with her MBA from the Haas School of Business at the University of California at Berkeley, she became one of the founding team members at Walmart.com. She then served as chief people officer at Peet's Coffee and Tea, an iconic Bay Area premium coffee company. Currently, Laila is the chief people officer for AllBirds, is an advisor to entrepreneurs and investors, and serves as a guest lecturer at Berkeley Law School.

Author photo © Gina Logan Photography

SELECTED TITLES FROM SHE WRITES PRESS

She Writes Press is an independent publishing company founded to serve women writers everywhere. Visit us at www.shewritespress.com.

Rethinking Possible: A Memoir of Resilience by Rebecca Faye Smith Galli. $16.95, 978-1-63152-220-8. After her brother's devastatingly young death tears her world apart, Becky Galli embarks upon a quest to recreate the sense of family she's lost—and learns about healing and the transformational power of love over loss along the way.

Where Have I Been All My Life? A Journey Toward Love and Wholeness by Cheryl Rice. $16.95, 978-1-63152-917-7. Rice's universally relatable story of how her mother's sudden death launched her on a journey into the deepest parts of grief—and, ultimately, toward love and wholeness.

Insatiable: A Memoir of Love Addiction by Shary Hauer. $16.95, 978-1-63152-982-5. An intimate and illuminating account of corporate executive—and secret love addict—Shary Hauer's migration from destructive to healthy love.

The Thriver's Edge: Seven Keys to Transform the Way You Live, Love, and Lead by Donna Stoneham. $16.95, 978-1-63152-980-1. A "coach in a book" from master executive coach and leadership expert Dr. Donna Stoneham, *The Thriver's Edge* outlines a practical road map to breaking free of the barriers keeping you from being everything you're capable of being.

Drop In: Lead with Deeper Presence and Courage by Sara Harvey Yao. $14.95, 978-1-63152-161-4. A compelling explanation about why being present is so challenging and how leaders can access clarity, connection, and courage in the midst of their chaotic lives, inside and outside of work.

People Leadership: 30 Proven Strategies to Ensure Your Team's Success by Gina Folk. $24.95, 978-1-63152-915-3. Longtime manager Gina Folk provides thirty effective ways for any individual managing or supervising others to reignite their team and become a successful—and beloved—people leader.